architecture

works and projects
# WARO KISHI
with an essay by masao furuyama

**Electa**architecture

720.8
K6/w

**editorial coordination**
Giovanna Crespi

**graphic design**
Tassinari/Vetta
(CODEsign)

**page layout**
Chiara Fasoli

**editing**
Gail Swerling

**cover graphics**
CODEsign

**technical coordination**
Mario Farè

**quality control**
Giancarlo Berti

Distributed by Phaidon Press
ISBN 1-904313-38-8

www.phaidon.com

www.electaweb.it

First published in English 2005

Printed in Hong Kong

# Contents

# The Architectural World of Waro Kishi
Masao Furuyama

# I

Waro Kishi is a leading Japanese Neomodernist. A most promising figure among the younger "next generation" architects who came to champion Neomodernism after the demise of Postmodernism, Kishi is one of very few Japanese architects who never joined ranks with the Postmodernist movement and hence garnered all the more acclaim when Japan's "bubble economy" burst in the early 1990s.

Kishi designs some of the most truly "architectural" buildings in the world today. Unlike the run of other architects who vie for attention with their "non-architectural" designs, he has kept on making real buildings characterized by a Euclidean clarity enhanced with a certain Japanese aesthetic refinement. The aesthetic qualities of Kishi's works speak for themselves: a quiet late-Modernist harmony, formally academic and conservative, yet at the same time studiously avoiding the pitfalls of arriviste avant-garde. The Postmodernists' pseudo-avant-garde self-destructed, but Kishi bravely chose to "bring up the rear," with an "après-garde" commitment to achieving a high-classicist perfection. While the "star" architects of the twentieth century were always avant-garde, the architects to watch in the twenty-first will surely emerge from the "après-garde." Kishi's works are masterpieces of an exactingly built order, distinguished by their expression of rational consistency and intellectual rigor. Not that they seek to challenge the quarrelsome ranks of the avant-garde's "masterpieces" and "triumphs": In this sense he may be seen as "bringing up the rear," though of course the great advantage is a happy liberation from the pressures of the "cutting edge." As a result, he gains a measure of objectivity, an analytic perspective or critical distance, as well as the courage to choose normal solutions. Better the ordinary than always the radical or eccentric, though at times this might even embody a middle-class aesthetic backed up by a healthy skepticism and common sense.

Unfortunately, unlike avant-garde aesthetics, après-garde aesthetics cannot offer a cathartic aesthetic kick. Very well, then, why on earth does Kishi's architecture thrill and inspire? First of all, by thorough analysis, he brings in formal vocabularies employed by modern architecture to lure the eye; that is, he incorporates a familiar Modernist gaze in his works and so succeeds in reversing shock-aesthetic catharsis back to a certain aesthetic nostalgia for Modernist architecture. His works, highly regarded for their intelligence and integrity, are composed of clear geometries, rationally systematized by spatial grammars and material rhetorics into extremely orthodox harmonies. The issue for him, then, is how to give such geometric spaces a personal flavor.

By in-depth study of Modernist architecture of the twenties, thirties and fifties, Kishi shows us how we still gaze longingly at the "good old" buildings of those now bygone decades. By adding in the modern tastes of those architects now regarded as historical masters, he transforms those "fearful geometries" without memory into nostalgic geometries; he subjectively rounds out the severity of their objective systems. Or to put it another way, he turns geometric space into a fantasy screen onto which the fans of mathematically formulated architecture can project their own imaginings. At the same time, this paradoxical "remembrance of things avant-garde" approach proves a liberation from architects' abiding "myth of originality" mindset, making it possible to view modern architecture as a subject for study or an exemplar for stylistic reference.

Some people may say that Kishi himself—his face, his physical frame—bears a striking resemblance to Mies van der Rohe in his later years, but the inclusion of "Asian tastes" and other pleasure-principle tendencies in his works evidences a certain distance from the Mies mainstream.

## II

Kishi possesses an almost too keenly analytic mind, and could easily have pursued an academic career. Likewise a car enthusiast, with an obvious bent for machines and all things mechanical, at one point he seemed well on the way to becoming an electrical engineer. Yet on the other hand, being rather poor at sports and disinclined to undergo the hardships of physical training, he showed tendencies toward epicureanism. Ultimately, Kishi, often seen as the techno-realist, developed a certain asceticism toward romantic adventure and sentimental literary tastes. In design, he prefers forms with a logical basis to over-expression of excess. The upshot is that Kishi's view of architecture, in its aim to provide aesthetic satisfaction by intellectual means, might well be described as classicist.

Kishi was born in 1950 into a doctor's family. Kishi's father, who ran a hospital in a small city on Japan's Inland Sea, had originally wanted to go into medical research, and was about to take a ship to America to study when he received word that his father was gravely ill, cutting short his dreams of training abroad. Kishi's younger brother later followed their father's medical vocation, leaving Kishi free to choose his own path in life; yet Kishi still wanted an academic post, if only to make up for his father's sacrifice. In 1969, amidst the student unrest of the times, Kishi entered Kyoto University. He earned an undergraduate degree in electrical engineering, then immediately switched over to architectural postgraduate studies, his sights now consciously set on becoming an architect. This was in 1973.

Kishi's student output seems full of late sixties' pop and super graphic expression: housing projects and primary schools that played mix-and-match with Venturi and Sterling and Charles Moore. Looking at these school-day tributes to his architect idols clearly shows he was an avid reader of the special-issue monographs in architectural magazines. They also present a different celebratory character from his later and more ascetic-looking works. Throughout his years of study, he enjoyed analyzing his favorite architectural figures and trends, showing an unparalleled talent for quickly absorbing and remaking all he learned. A careful examination reveals no drawing upon the cranky concepts and unbuilt theoretics of Superstudio. No, the architects he looked up to were excessive, effusive, ebullient . . .

Architecture was fun! Design was not for brooding!

While working for his Masters degree, Kishi conducted a historical survey of modern architecture, followed by his 1978 thesis, a formal analysis of the work of architect Kameki Tsuchiura; he applied such analytical models as Colin Rowe's "transparency" and Peter Eisenman's analyses of Giuseppe Terragni's Casa del Fascio (1932–33) to the achievements of Tsuchiura, often considered the pinnacle of Japanese Modernism. This also led to Kishi's later concerns by way of a prolonged interest in formative operations that were to underscore his own design methodologies. Thereafter, while still looking for architects he liked, he pressed on into the realm of experimental psychology, studying the relationship between the manipulation of geometric forms and how they affect spatial perception. When, in around 1975, perhaps inspired by the so-called "Neo-Corbusian" New York Five, Kishi began to see himself in the mold of a New-Miesian; almost as if Corbu : Richard Meier = Mies : Kishi. The reason was that having already studied almost all there was to research about Le Corbusier, that only left Mies van der Rohe. Just then, Kishi's biggest concern, his biggest worry, was his need for a "partner."

After postgraduate studies at Kyoto University, he worked for three years in Masayuki Kurokawa's office in Tokyo, interning in architecture, interior decor and product design. During that time, he still pursued his own architectural studies on the side, publishing co-translations of Rob Krier's *Stadtraum in Theorie und Praxis* (1975) in 1980 and Reyner Banham's *Design by Choice* (1981) in 1983.

In 1981, he took a teaching position in Kyoto, and he moved from Tokyo to Kyoto. Soon after, however, he fell seriously ill, which proved a major turning point and strengthened his lifelong commitment to architecture. Awaking to his "mission in life," he immersed himself in study and work with overriding energy. In fact he made it his duty to take annual architectural survey trips to America and Europe, the findings from which he published a book *Case Study House* in 1997. At the same time he rediscovered his favorite architects: Kameki Tsuchiura, Sutemi Horiguchi, A. Lurçat, Robert Mallet-Stevens, J.J.P. Oud, Gerrit Rietvelt, L.C. van der Vlugt, Richard Neutra, Charles and Ray Eames, Rudolf M. Schindler and Marcel Breuer. Another important aspect of this period was his discovery of Miami Art Déco, a school of Modernist taste he promptly went to research firsthand, an effort which helped him establish the final navigational coordinates of his own architectural world—and which ultimately led to Kishi's works being acclaimed for their place in architectural history.

Kishi's Classicist period works are characterized by a well-harmonized Modernist aesthetic. Not blown by the winds of late twentieth century Postmodernism but remaining aloof, he continued his pursuit of highly-perfected, rational beauty. In particular the works between 1980 and 1995 stand out in Kishi's oeuvre for what might be called their Classicist period spatial qualities.


## III
There are no shadows in Kishi's architecture. Either in the metaphoric or the physical sense, Kishi's buildings are visibly brighter; the spaces he creates are clear and fresh as a Sunday morning. This comes as the result of their rigorously logical geometries, whose application serves to imbue simple generated space with a certain naivety, immaculateness and innocence. In a word, this is real abstraction: the greatest virtue of Kishi's architecture is its highly moral and proper spatial order informed by a rational consistency. Yet even so, what we generally look for in architecture is not rational order so much as inspiring spaces, just as we might expect a poem to go beyond the literal meaning of the poet's words. If reason is to provoke an emotional response it must transcend reason. Likewise, in order for geometry to attain true beauty, it must attain a realm of catharsis beyond mere mathematics—and in the case of Kishi's architecture, a catharsis beyond logic, rejecting both radical austerities and eccentric tensions. Neither his intellect nor his aesthetics would allow that. Kishi turns his back on hard-sell appeal and cheap bravura forms, assuming a more moderate predilection for abstraction that might be termed his "personal mean." The essence of Kishi's abstract vision thus emerges as a uniquely quiescent innocence suffused with clarity and optimism.

Over the last decade of the twentieth century, the interplay between social change and changes in architecture has been little short of amazing. Back in 1990, when Japanese society was riding high on the bubble, an economy bloated to a dangerous degree, unimaginable in America or Europe, building also enjoyed a boom; architecture went to extremes of shape and decoration—the heyday of Postmodern styling—to match the giddy atmosphere prevailing through the country. But then the bubble burst, and everything suddenly went quiet; the Postmodern festival was over,å leaving a vacuum in its wake. Whereupon, in keeping with the subdued mood of society, a new architecture came to the fore: a trend I call Neomodernism. Clean and sober, it signified a return to an orthodox modern line. In contrast to Postmodernism's more sculptural digression away from pure built form, Neomodernism sought to recover a true architectural essence.

From 1995 on, Waro Kishi may be regarded at the leading proponent of this tendency. Self-effacing, toning down all flamboyant color to an aesthetic monotone, he brought architectural qualities back to architecture. His works are pure, humble and beautiful, qualities that propelled him all at once to center stage when society's values reversed post-bubble. Cleaving to readily appreciated Modernist images—the very things that Postmodernism had attacked—Kishi creates an architecture of such refinement as to make his works the epitome of Neomodernism.

His Sonobe SD Office (1993) exemplifies these qualities. Situated in suburban Kyoto, the project attaches great importance to its yard space. The precise placing of the glass-walled office building and bold steel bridge transform an otherwise vacant site into a perambulatory Cubist garden, where the white perpendiculars of handrails throughout demarcate the entire zone with their crisp, severe geometry. The sensitive handling of the skeletal steel frame of the building itself leans somehow toward traditional Japanese *sukiya* sensibilities, while the granite floor and expansive glass façades recall the refined tastes of Mies van der Rohe's designs.

Likewise his house in Shimogamo (1994) is a masterpiece of orthodox Modernism. Breaking out of the boxlike mold of his earliest works, the sharply aligned steel frame makes for a nice "al dente" expression of geometric ratios that extend to the very edges of the site, creating a unifying visual order and clarity throughout. A most elegant "lady" among Kishi's steel-framed works.

Only a very small minority in architectural circles today dare to stay truly orthodox, and that rarity makes their works all the more valuable. Kishi's orthodoxy is visualised in careful

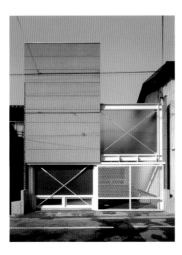

geometric harmonies between the parts and the whole. Highly rational, but quiet in taste. Avoiding both oversimplification and heavily centripetal concentration, he designs without bringing too much of the idiosyncratic auteur to the fore. In some senses, then, Kishi's Neo-modernist aesthetic perfectly coincided with the tides of post-bubble Neo-Conservatism.

Kishi's first built work was Kim House (1987). A strong influence from Tadao Ando's Row House in Sumiyoshi (1976) is clearly in evidence, as is a watchful eye on Toyo Ito. If "debut" works like these can be said to spell out the basic profile of any given architect, then Kim House and the Row House in Sumiyoshi demand incisive comparison. Here I wish to place particular emphasis on the differences so as to highlight the special characteristics of Kishi's architecture.

Row House in Sumiyoshi: First, giving the façade an objective once-over, we observe a symmetrical, largely door-shaped composition in which the actual door occupies a central position. Only two upright rectangular shapes are used—the overall outline and the door—while the three-element scheme applied throughout the building is echoed in the long-short-long, or rather wall-opening-wall rhythm of the façade.

Kim House: Having roughly the same dimensions, this can be considered a translation of the concrete Row House in Sumiyoshi into a steel-frame structure. The façade is composed of unit panels approximately 90 centimeters square, arranged in three rows of three on the ground floor (minus three for the door) and again on the upper floor (minus two for the window). The simple 1:2 proportion of the window and 3:1 proportion of the door give clear visual expression to a mathematical relationship, the ratio of natural numbers as simple fractions.

Row House in Sumiyoshi: In general, three-element schemes and symmetry are said to belong to the grammar of Classicist architecture. The Row House in Sumiyoshi cannot, however, be wholly explained by any such classical models, and that is its appeal. A faceless wall perhaps, yet it is not simply geometry; there is something almost archaic to its solidity.

Kim House: The grouting between the panels serves to underscore the geometric ratios. The doorway, however, is placed asymmetrically, and a wider variety of materials is used: steel structure, aluminum sashes, and painted flexible board panels. Whereas Ando's signature concrete gives the Row House in Sumiyoshi a sculptural plasticity, the materials at Kim House render a more anonymous and generic "cool" finish.

Row House in Sumiyoshi: The featureless wall caused a stir among the local neighborhood community when it first appeared, but after the initial shock they soon grew

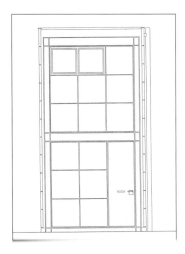 

accustomed to it. People want to read undue meanings into it because the wall presents such a total blank-effectively a screen for projecting imaginings. Obviously a wall fetishism, causing architecture obsessives to fixate as much on what is not there as what is. What in psychoanalytic terms might be addressed as "transference" or "mirroring."

Kim House: On other real life fronts, the problem of rain falling into the courtyard is solved by judicious placing of the deck. The stairs are also more natural and easier to negotiate. A comparison of the geometrically rational harmonies of Kim House with the more self-assertive Row House in Sumiyoshi reveals that geometry plays an opposite role in each; the excessive pose of Row House in Sumiyoshi is at odds with what the author would call the "equal beauty" of Kim House.

As also appears from his later works, Kishi opts for emblematic odd-even geometric ratios (even multiples of odd fractions like 2:3 or 2:5) so as to transcend simple symmetries and elicit a more Japanese sense of visual balance, while typically employing repeated elements to underscore the proportional design solution. Only next, within that scheme, does Kishi use symmetry to render an order of part to part. Because of this avoidance of extremes of centripetally encompassed configuration, those parts alone emerge as harmoniously Modernist.

In the heyday of Postmodernism Kishi's architecture was sprinkled with visual enticements in the form of nostalgic design elements from early Modernism. Although in fact, viewers tended to look beyond the immediate works to afterimages of an irretrievable past.

Waro Kishi's Kim House (1987) stands a decade after Ando's Row House in Sumiyoshi (1976), though equally a decade before Miyamoto's Zenkai House ("Devastated House") built in the aftermath of the great 1995 Kobe Earthquake. These three works are responses to three successive generations of late capitalist society: first generation, an autonomous individual pursuing his own egoistic ideal; second generation, a heteronomous organization man seeking acclaim from others; third generation, a pathological narcissist, symptoms commonly seen in Japanese in recent years. Ando's Row House in Sumiyoshi was a masterpiece among the so-called "guerrilla houses" of his youth, an assertion to Ando's view of urban life as struggle: If life is struggle, then architecture also has to be struggle; where there is no struggle there can be no passion, and where the passions are not stirred no great works are born. The autonomous solitary self accepts no compromises, for it is through the fight that one establishes oneself as an individual and as an architect. By contrast the next generation Kim House emulates the famously mute and mysterious "Sumiyoshi façade," so as to project

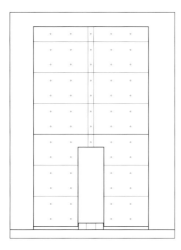

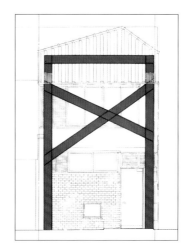

its own architectural idea. Architect Waro Kishi grew up admiring the strong expression of "Sumiyoshi," so he was perhaps inevitably ambitious to one day create his own version of the house. Or to borrow from Lacanian psychology, the Kim House is like a bright child emerging from protective nurture to "mirror" the role model of a strong father.

Coming to the next generation, however, Miyamoto's Zenkai House, registers wholly off the architectural scale. A properly pathological narcissist gesture, it comes as a slap in the face of any architect who adheres to the tacit ego-ideal that creation must be aesthetic, must be "architectural." Completely ignoring all paternal orders to "build beautifully," the fractured steel and brick walls remain in place as dysfunctional fragments. Like some news photo of a war orphan staring intently into the face of destruction, this woodframe house hit by the January 1995 Kobe Earthquake was "revived" by adding an absurdly sturdy steel frame, as if to give excessive evidence of its injuries by means of equally scarring reparative surgery. As if proclaiming that architecture's expected social role of making things as "good as new" after a disaster and returning disrupted life to a healthy norm, trying to heal wounds by shoring up the shocks architecturally, is an impossibility.

Comparing the three works, both Row House in Sumiyoshi and Zenkai House make strong individualistic statements, Kim House is altogether straightforward in its expression. Unlike the "Sumiyoshi's" angry scowl or Zenkai's painful tears, Kim House just smiles, perky as a kid playing football. Where Row House in Sumiyoshi comes across as autistic and uncommunicative, where the Zenkai house glares back at us in mournful spite, the Kim House seems cheerful and fresh as a wholesome young boy. Kim House conveys nothing so much as a positive stance of trying to maximize the happiness of the common man. Prior to 1995, Kishi's values were centered on the well-being of the group; or to put it another way, he often depended on friends and fellow architects' advice so as to fully respond to the expectations and ideals of those outside the profession, and hence he himself endeavored to resemble the ideal understanding other. For as in sports and in art, mimicking others actually helps to improve skills and to attain an identity; more specifically, you first learn to recognize yourself in an external mirror image, then discern whether or not that image loves you, then drink in its milk as sustenance, the mirror image now internalized.

After 1995, however, the winds of world architecture shifted. For in that fateful year of earthquake in Kobe, all at once the bubble burst, the earthquake, Postmodernism faltered—and Kishi's fortunes changed. His time had come. How could society-wide disasters herald a single architect's "arrival"?

The first factor was that Japanese society had tired of all the clamorous Postmodern forms born of economic excess. On the threshold of economic decline, the first thing to be jettisoned was over-the-top styling; Japanese society turned away from Postmodernism and sought something more succinct and frugal. Kishi's aesthetics answered these subliminal needs.

The second factor, even more cogent than the first, is that when views toward architecture change it is typically not due to any variance in content but rather to an arbitrary ranking. The dramatic reappraisal of Kishi may thus be summarized in the statement, "Truth is a place." Any work of architecture in itself is merely a referent, which some historical accident just happens to place right at the very center of attention so as to occupy the seat of truth in people's minds. This phenomenon is very close to that of fetishism, a fixation upon tangential objects, as in when a man desires a woman's high heels in place of the woman herself. Kishi's architecture makes no point of loud expression or profound messages. But his architecture finds a place in people's desire.

The third factor proved the ultimate reason. Around this time, Kishi brought out a wave of works intentionally imbued with references to masterpieces of Modernist architectural history—here a refined version of an avant-garde villa, there an "upgrade" of a B-class Modernist house. Not just replicated Modernist architecture, in other words, meta-Modernist architecture, that allows us to see through his creations to the afterimages behind. Most notably, we see hints of Kishi's "core vision" of Modernism through his use of steel framing, as if Kishi were erecting works to frame the "great masters."

This touches upon the important issue of the relative positioning of architects among themselves. When we laypersons overview the "great master" architects and those architects who then analyzed them, lining them up far-to-near like a solar system, we inevitably cause eclipse effects. The more those core figures behind Kishi's vision increase in number and luminance, the more they backlight Kishi's works to the point where they dazzle our layperson's eyes. What is important at this juncture, then, is the positioning of Mies relative to Kishi relative to ourselves. We may be looking straight at a work by Kishi, but the sheer weight and power of Mies's works directly behind forms a splendid halo around Kishi. The objects of Kishi's esteem shine straight through his eyes to ours and speak to us. The exalted objects of Kishi's reverence are thus both in Kishi's works and in the background, which serves as a "special effect," allowing Kishi's works to take on Modernist features.

Kishi's architecture is a sort of Modernism in an age when Modernism has all but disappeared, in an age when the works of pure Modernism can only be viewed at a nostalgic distance as lost and gone. Our age today is one in which we can no longer see the appeal of pure Modernist architecture directly; ours is an adulation of Modernist architecture seen through nostalgic eyes. In this sense, we should see Kishi as the discoverer of a nostalgic gaze toward modern architecture, a visionary who successfully transforms our quest for catharsis into a fond nostalgia. By merging with modern architecture—though such mergers are generally regarded as a primary stage of emotional bonding with another—and reducing the objects of his infatuation to signs so as to merge in toto, Kishi reifies a love affair with all things Modernist.

For indeed, to Kishi, Modernist architecture is a state of mind, a symptom of longing that will always go on seeking surrogates once the object of adulation is lost. In fact, Kishi's works resemble one another in this regard: like subtle variations on a common theme orchestrated in clear geometries, Kishi performs his Modernist fugue over and over again, playing back afterimages of long lost modern masterpieces while steadily refining and stylizing his own creations.

**IV**

With the year 2001 as the threshold to his Art Déco period, we note a change in Kishi's style into what clearly seems to be a certain fondness for Postmodernism. As if he wished to play the pure Modernist less, dabbling in a bit of naff but by now nostalgic Postmodernism. Not to speak of formative aspects like brash colors or materials or textures, someday this is sure to be called Kishi's Art Déco period.

Kishi seems bent on undermining the harmonious vision he's built up to now and starting to experiment toward a new self. In his most recent works, we observe a tendency toward placing fetishistic objects directly within abstract geometries: Asian bric-à-brac collected on his travels or fragments on B-class Modernism, all extracted from their native historical contexts and brought into the contemporary Japanese house. The technique is one of mythologizing by means of transplanting objects of nostalgia into the present as archaeological relics. Indeed, it was Postmodernism that brought such mythologization to bear upon B-class Modernism. Thus Kishi's architectural vision may appear to have moved from "sacred" meta-Modernism to "profane" Postmodernism, but this merely corresponds to a shift in his methodological interests from abstract space to concrete materials, from the beauty of emptiness to the nitty-gritty of things. He is experimenting, mixing dark opaque material into clear bright space, trying to see which materials will melt into space, which forms and colors will blend into geometry. Up to now his greatest concern was the creation of abstract space; making architecture was nothing more nor less than using concrete materials to create abstract spaces. For while in theory color and texture, all sense of physical presence, must be eliminated in order to heighten the quotient of abstractness (without mentioning that Kishi always sought pure spaces unmitigated by extraneous admixtures), lately he has been intentionally experimenting with including walls and columns of various colors, textures and masses, expressions of non-abstractable material essences. Within those processes where space and material interact, the active implementation of inert materials that resist dissolving into space can be savored as a small dose of invigorating disruption to the systematic order of things.

At the same time, judging by how he handles those material aspects, counter to prevailing misconceptions of Kishi's architecture as minimalist—where Minimalism asymptotically reduces architectural qualities to cold geometry, thereby eroding all architecture-like expression—Kishi conversely preserves a modicum of form. He lets the eaves slip out of line, implementing such details for delicately expressive effect. Most recently, however, the material aspects that attract his interest are those that resist fusing into the symbolic nexus of architecture. What are they? In Lacanian psychoanalytic terms, those residual elements that cannot be rendered symbolically are indelible fragments of the real world; that is, fragments of reified material reality and as such tantamount to one's own corporeal being, pieces of one's past self encountered in the process of re-examining traumatic narratives. The materials Kishi introduces into his works may include resurgent pop icons from his youth. In that sense, he has now returned to the epicureanism and optimism of his student years, and is simply enjoying designing architecture. And the outcome of these experiments? Surely his will be a richly formative vision. Or else he may well instill Modernist architecture with a "forbidden garden" of decoration. Call it Postmodernism, call it Art Déco, he will seek out the pleasure principles that lie beyond. Not that he would pursue pleasure to the exclusion of happiness. He continues to be an architect pursuing an ideal architecture uniting beauty and happiness.

Waro Kishi designs some of the most truly "architectural" buildings in the world today. Unlike the run of other architects who try to stand out with their "non-architectural" designs, he has persistently sought intelligent, beautiful and skillful architectural spaces, real buildings of Euclidean geometric clarity infused with refined Kyoto sensibilities.

detached houses

# Kim House

Ikuno, Osaka 1986–87

This small house is located in one of Osaka's downtown areas, where the streets are lined with row houses on pre-war lots interspersed with factories and warehouses. To build it, part of a row house was removed. On the site thus created, a double-deck steel building (with a frontage of one bay of 2.58 meters and a depth of three bays of 5.40 meters) was erected with a small courtyard at its center. The floors of both the courtyard and the dining room are covered with white tiles, so both areas form a single space without distinction between indoors and outdoors, when the doors between them are fully opened.

To achieve the highest possible degree of factory production, a special method (similar to prefabrication) was devised, reducing on-site work to a minimum. First, four wide-flange steel frames were erected at equal intervals along the length of the rectangular lot. Then, the floor of the upper story and the concrete foundations were completed. With this, the frame was finished. All that was required next was to attach molded cement panels and aluminum windows and doors to the frame, using curtain-wall techniques.

The project was carried out under extremely difficult conditions, as the lot was small and the budget was tight. However this did not harm the building's design; in fact it taught me that such difficulties can actually stimulate the imagination.

Axonometric projection of the house open on west side.

Interior of the court with the second-floor landing linking the two bedrooms.

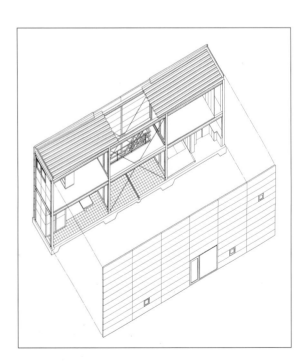

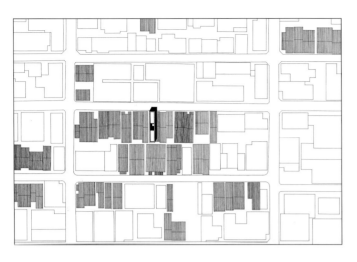

Site map; plans of the second and ground floors and longitudinal section.

Detail of the stairs, view of the court towards the tatami room and principal façade facing north.

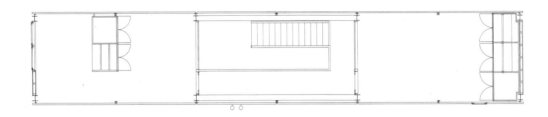

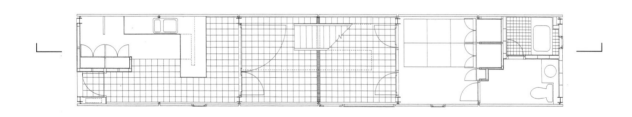

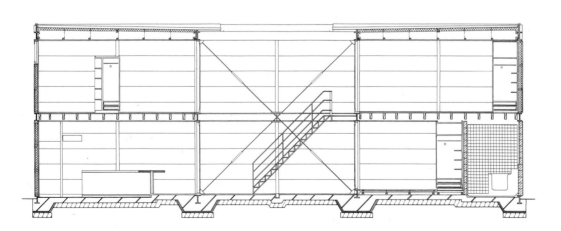

# House in Nipponbashi
Naniwa, Osaka 1990–92

The house was built on an extremely small plot of land in downtown Osaka. The façade of the building, 2.50 meters wide, fills the entire front of the site. The house is 13 meters deep, and the lower three floors were kept as low as possible. This construction is topped by the uppermost floor, which contains the dining room. With a ceiling 6 meters high, the dining room occupies no less than two-thirds of the entire building; the remaining third of the depth is filled by an open-air terrace. The result is that the structure not only emphasizes the vertical direction but takes full advantage of the depth of the narrow site. The building has two main themes. One is the verticality of urban life. The other is the creation of a floating living space (the top floor) that is cut off from the noise of the street and close to Nature.

Achieving this required nothing more than a few square meters of terrace space and just 30 square meters of building space, including the generous dining room. What I tried to do in designing this house was to give new meaning to the concept of a roof garden.
If modern architecture can be called revolutionary, then it is partly because it abolished the roof. Before that the roof was an indispensable part of any architectural creation. With the advent of modern architecture, however, the roof disappeared. That, at least, appears to be the significance of the invention of the roof garden. If so, I wondered, what does this space called the roof garden mean to us? What is its significance?
Take, for instance, Le Corbusier's Beistegui House in Paris facing the Champs Elysées. The house was

planned to be topped by a penthouse. Among the salient features of this building is the view it affords, which puts the observer at the same height as the Arc de Triomphe. At the same time, however, the observer finds himself in an elevated outdoor space that appears to be at ground level. In other words, the building creates in the observer both the sensation of a privileged view and a unique feeling of being afloat. That, I think, is the precious quality that was made possible by the modern concept of space, or more specifically the roof garden.
I do not know whether this house with its tiny terrace and dining room can be called a work of modern architecture. However, I am convinced that there is one thing we need to avoid, and that is to be blind to what our age has wrought.

Axonometric projection of the house showing the principal system of vertical connection.

Internal stairs facing the street to the east.

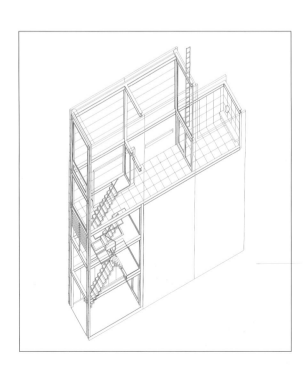

Site map and plans of the second and ground floors.

Longitudinal and cross sections and plans of the fourth and third floors.

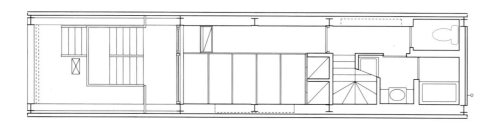

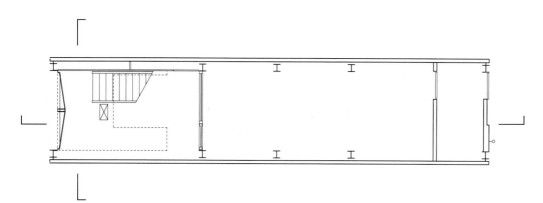

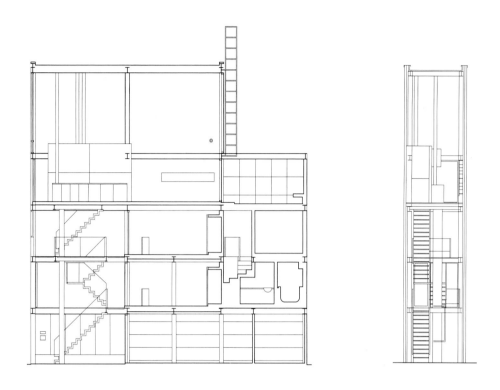

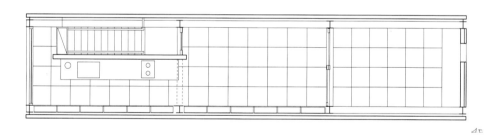

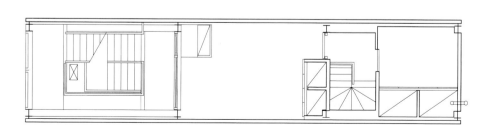

Views of dining room and terrace on the top floor.

The east façade.

## House in Shimogamo
Sakyo, Kyoto 1992–94

This two-story house is located in an urban area at the foot of the Kitayama mountains in the northern part of Kyoto. Covering almost the entire site, the house is two bays measuring 3.20 meters each wide and three bays of 4.0 meters each deep. At the core of the steel-frame structure, I created an inner court measuring one bay by two bays in plan. The rest of the house consists of a steel frame with external walls made of formed cement plates, steel window frames, and gate doors. In designing this house, I was fully aware that contemporary urban houses seem real only to the extent that they are unique solutions to a number of fixed preconditions. Nevertheless, I made an attempt to develop, not just a specific solution, but a prototype of the urban house of the kind that has been a dream of twentieth-century Modernism. I therefore concentrated on incorporating new ideas into the planning and structure, which were the most important aspects of modern architecture.

In designing the house, privacy was not my main concern. Instead I focused on the relationship between the external space—meaning the inner court—and the rooms facing onto it. The result is a large three-dimensional living space, with individual rooms that are independent yet interrelated. Nor was I concerned too much with the structure. Instead, I treated it as merely one of the basic elements from which the whole is assembled, in order to create the effect of a single functional unit. It seems to me that, several decades having passed since the heroic age of modern architecture, the time has come to reconsider the implications of the machine age for architecture.

Axonometric projection.

View of court and dining room from the bedroom.

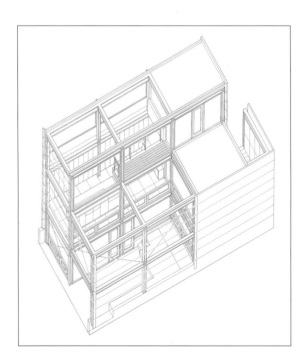

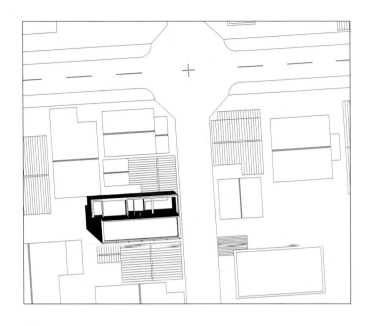

Site map and plan of the second and ground floors.

Section through the court, longitudinal sections and west and north elevations.

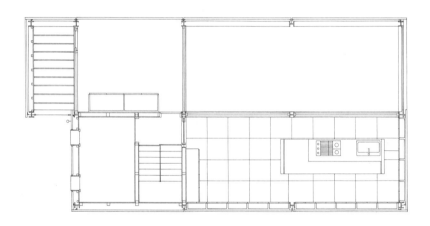

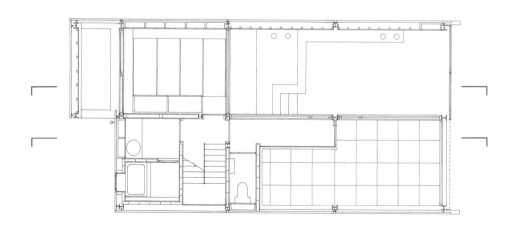

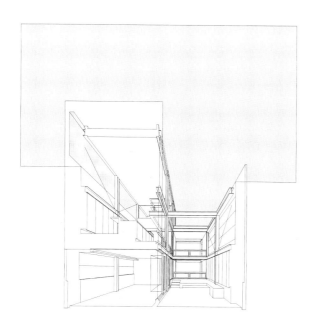

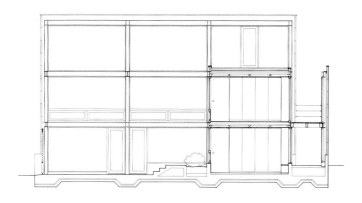

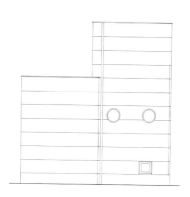

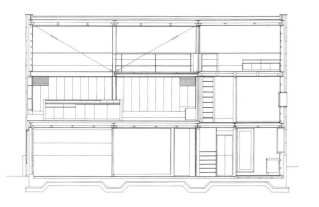

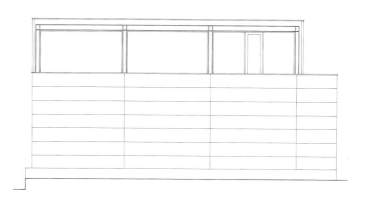

View of the east front;
constructional details
of the façade system and a
structural node on the court.

Dining room/kitchen with
the study at far end and court
on the right.

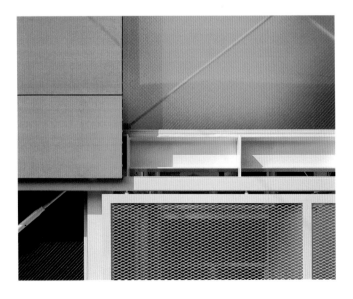

## House in Higashi-Osaka
Osaka, 1995–97

This house is not a heroic expression of contemporary technology and industrial products. Instead, it has been constructed by cladding a structural steel frame with molded cement panels and installing steel window frames.

The theme that I explored in the design was the potential of mainstream industrial vernacular. Therefore, the house, is the complete antithesis of a monolithic, one-of-a-kind building made of reinforced concrete. It is a type of structure that anyone could build anywhere in the world.

Taking the same approach as I took in the House at Nipponbashi, I used commonly available methods to arrive at a solution that is unique to this site, situation, and environment. The building stands in a suburb of Osaka, in a monotonous residential district sliced through by private railway lines. The site, located close to a bustling shopping street that leads to a railway station, is surrounded by condominiums and has only two elevations, one facing another house and the other facing the street. These are conditions that are typical of a Japanese metropolitan suburb.

The main structure has a frontage of two 3.60 meter bays and a depth of three 3.40 meter bays. A staircase and terrace occupy an area one bay square on the side facing the street.

Behind the main structure, another area one-bay square is given over to a court with a stairway. This court is open on the south side at the top, and that is the only opening on the south side in the entire building. The court gives access to the third-floor living/dining room, which has a 4.0-meter high ceiling.

Part of the roof is translucent, and this serves to orchestrate the transition from the court to the interior space. The main floor is only a few meters above ground, yet this slight difference in elevation produces a distinctive space that is at once removed from the city and, at the same time, open to it.

Axonometric projection.

View looking from the court towards the terrace and dining room.

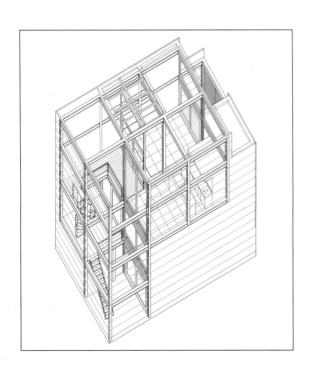

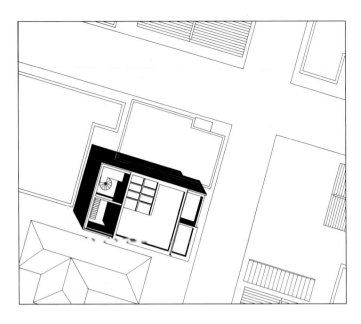

Site map and plans of the ground floor, third and second floors.

Longitudinal section and east and south elevations.

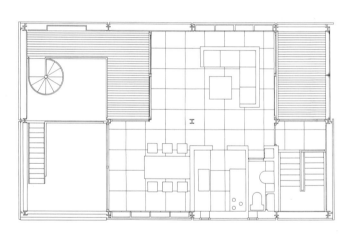

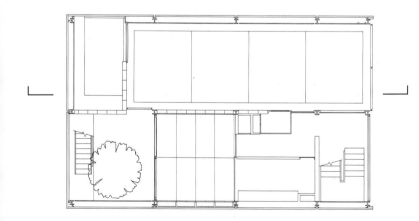

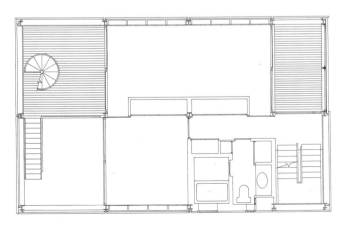

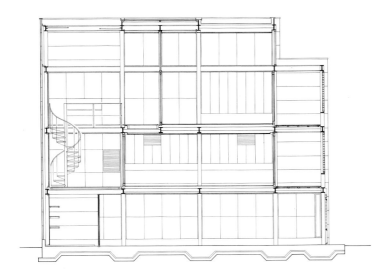

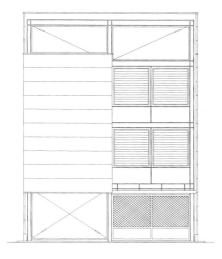

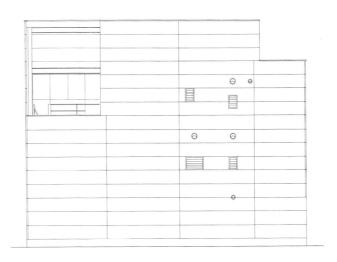

East front and detail
of the façade system.

View from the living room
towards the terrace.

## House in Suzaku
Nara 1996–98

A house in a newly developed residential area on the outskirts of Nara. The basic elements are two separate 9 by 5.40 meter volumes staggered in height and connected by a slope. The composition means that one volume on the east side contains the public areas: living, dining and the roof garden; while one volume in the west contains the private areas: bedrooms and a tea ceremony room. In between these volumes is the courtyard which provides natural greenery and prevents a direct view from one volume to the other because of the staggered height of the volumes. The house is a courtyard type, but it is not intended to reject the city, but to have a controlled openness. This is achieved through the wooden louver walls that protect the glass surface of the awning window louvers. These give depth to the outside space in relation to the townscape. With these the garden assumes two faces: a semi-closed one in relation to the townscape and an open, liberating one for the interior space of the house, while also enhancing the character of the private spaces.

East-west section.

View of the entrance from south-west.

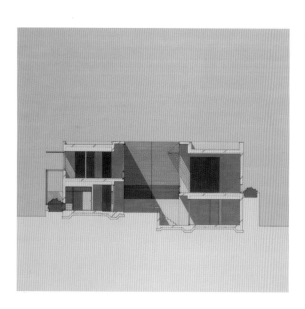

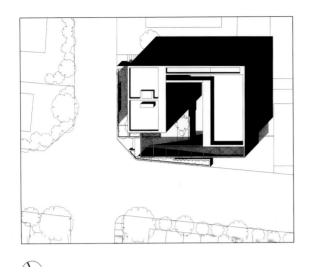

Site map, plans of the ground and
second floors and south elevation.

Detailed east-west section
and north-south section.

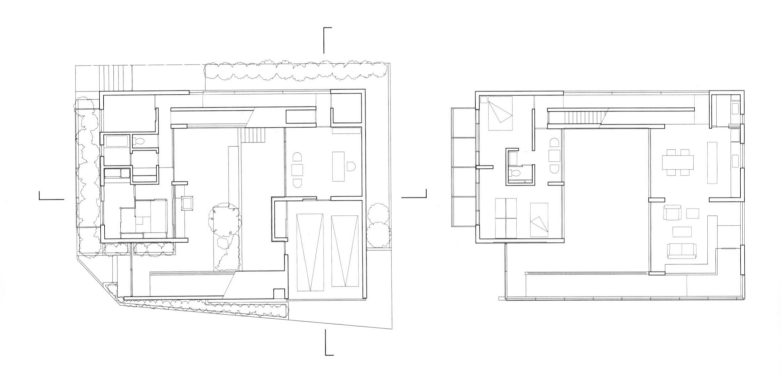

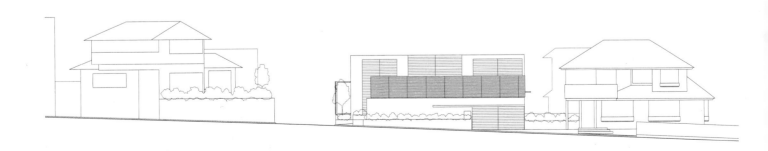

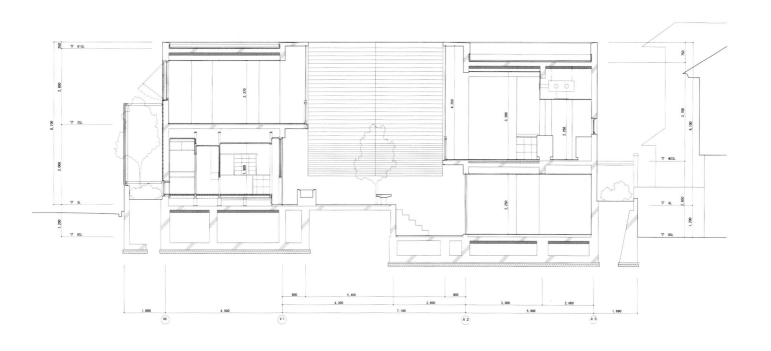

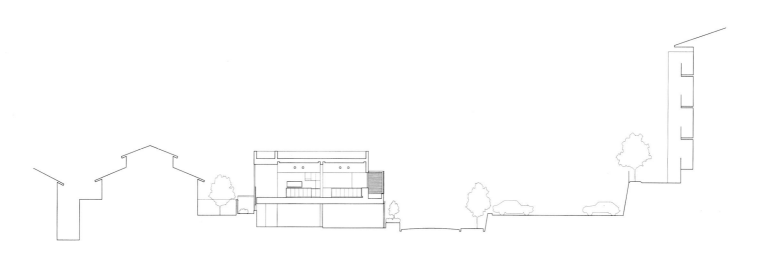

**43**

Views of the internal court from south and from the living/dining room on the second floor.

Living room with the court on the right; view from the ramp between ground and second floors; tea room with the court in the background.

# House in Kurakuen I
Nishinomiya, Hyogo 1996–98

The site is quite special. It is on the southern side of a slope facing a valley. The main road is 3 meters higher than the highest part of the slope. From the main road there is a panoramic view of the green valley below. Because of these unique conditions, I tried to limit the volume of the house as much as possible in order to blend the façade into the scenery.

The highest level of the house is set on the same level as the main road and is the most public space. From there a stairway leads down to the semi-public area, namely the living room and dining room, and below that are the private quarters, meaning the bedrooms. Each level of the house is a distinctive space. All the rooms face and are connected to external terraces and gardens, and this creates a feeling of being afloat in the natural environment of the house. There is a hierarchical sequence of spaces, from the living and dining room and the half-enclosed space of the terrace to the open valley below. One is made immediately aware of the changing seasons and the movement of the sun. The house provides a rare opportunity for a city-dweller to immerse himself in nature.

East-west section.

View of the terrace with the living/dining room on the left.

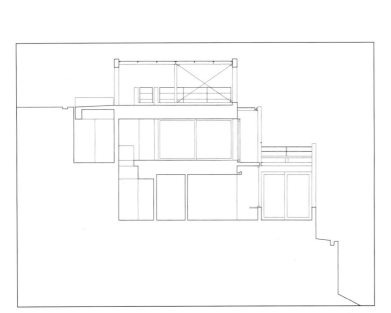

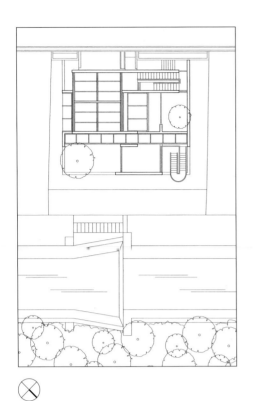

Site map; plans of second,
ground and third floors
and north elevation.

Views of west façade and
the terrace with the living/dining
area at right.

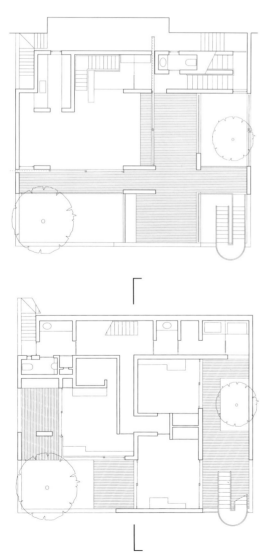

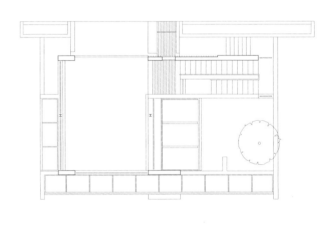

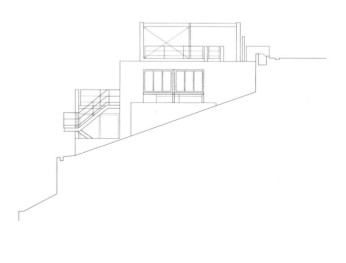

## House in Kurakuen II
Nishinomiya, Hyogo 1996–2001

The site is a special one in the Hanshin area, a sloping residential district facing the sea, and the terrain rises from the road by 7 meters with an ascending gradient of around 30 degrees. From this site there is a view of the entire residential area, the sprawling cityscape of the suburbs of Osaka and over the bay. It is possible to view the entire scene in one sweep. So the first issue in this project is how to deal with the special landscape.

I created two blocks with a floating reinforced steel structure. On the left are the private quarters, while on the right is the public living/dining quarters. The two areas are linked by a sloping ramp. The roof of the topmost floor on the left-hand block containing the individual rooms is made to appear as thin as possible. To dramatize living in the air, continuous horizontal windows are used together with an adjoining terrace. For the two-story living/dining block the usual move would be to have huge two-story openings, but I opted for the opposite. Instead, I decided to use small openings that explore ways of framing the view. I feel that it is an effective approach to somehow reverse the standard thinking. The upshot is that in the private rooms the view is wide open, while by contrast in the living and dining area the view is framed.

Axonometric section.

View of living-room terrace with dining-room window on the left.

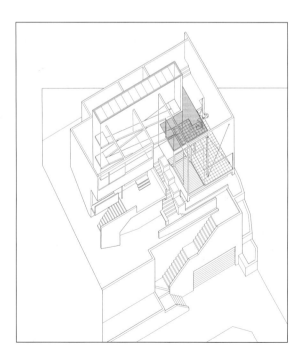

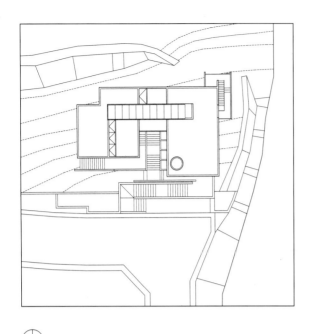

Site map, plans of ground
and second floors, longitudinal
and cross sections.

East, north and south elevations.

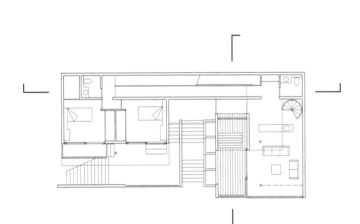

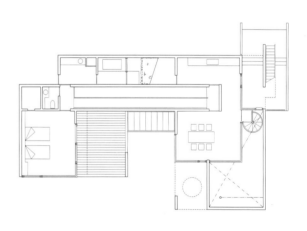

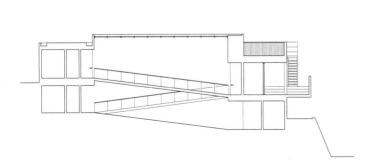

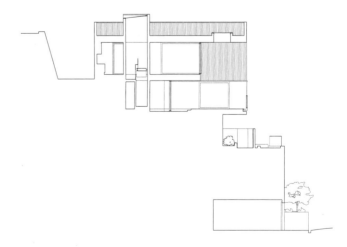

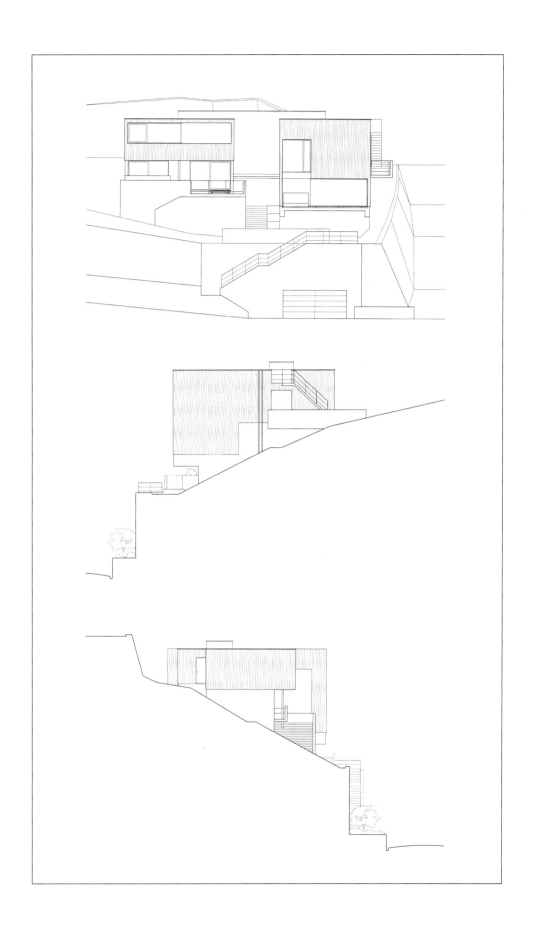

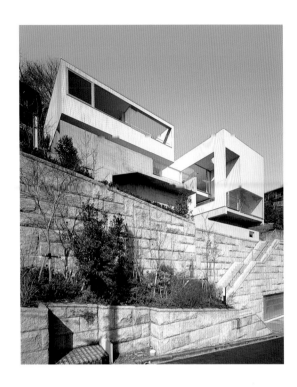

Part of the east façade and view of the dining room looking towards the terrace.

Living room with the large dining-room window and the spiral staircase leading to the upper floor; living room with the spiral staircase, dining room with a view outside.

# House in Fukaya

Saitama 1999–2001

This house is located in Fukaya, Saitama Prefecture on the north Kanto plain. Despite its proximity to megalopolitan Tokyo, the site is encompassed by monotonous, semi-urban surroundings, typical of north Kanto—a setting that discourages description as a "city suburb."

For this location I proposed a house having a closed attitude towards its surroundings and an internal court. I chose a closed configuration because in these surroundings I sensed a stark atmosphere quite remote from the image usually associated with a domicile. What was needed, I thought, was a building closed to such surroundings yet open in its interior space. The house has a rectangular plan measuring 9.60 meters east to west and 23.40 meters north to south and is tripartite in function. The south part contains the private elements—the garage and bedrooms—laid out on two levels. The north part, which is a half-level higher in elevation, contains the living/dining area: a large space with a ceiling height of 4.50 meters. A court with a pool is placed between them in the center of the building. The court serves as a link between the south and north parts, which are staggered in elevation, while yet separating them. The court also functions as an external living room, for it is designed to form a unit with the living/dining area. To give this court continuity with the living/dining area, I sought to minimize the dimensions of the intervening structure. By absorbing the horizontal thrusts into the external wall structure, I was able to use freestanding posts measuring just 6 × 100 centimeters. The glazing is attached directly to these posts, so that they are free from window sash as well as from wall structure.

By using factory materials and leaving the stark structural details visible, I gave the building architectural character. This may sound paradoxical. Yet, the way to confront those stark surroundings, I felt, was not by presenting a space replete with the warmth of congenial materials but rather an aggressive deployment of the kinds of materials and structures that proliferate in the surroundings.

Axonometric section.

View of the swimming pool and internal court towards the dining/living area.

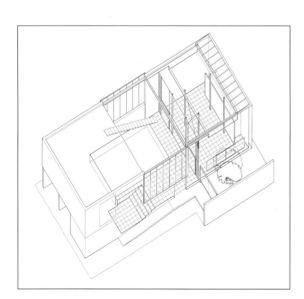

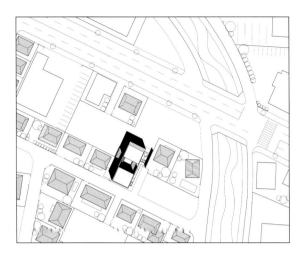

Site map and plans of second and ground floors.

Exploded axonometric section of the constructional system and south elevation.

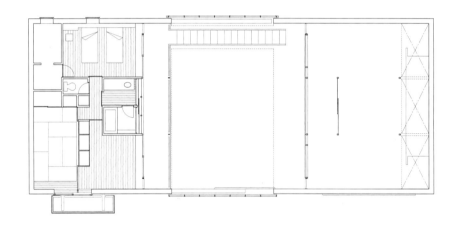

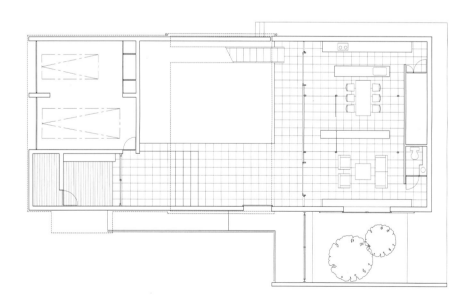

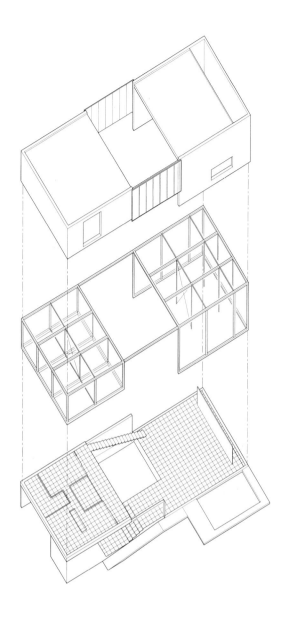

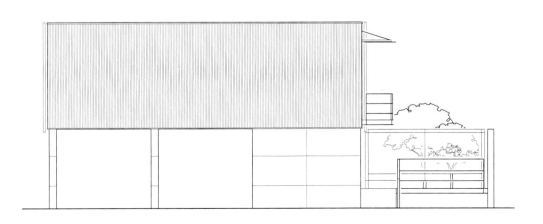

East and south façades.

Views of the living/dining area.

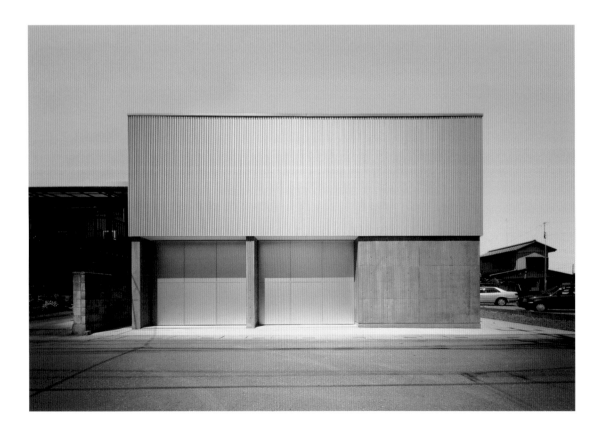

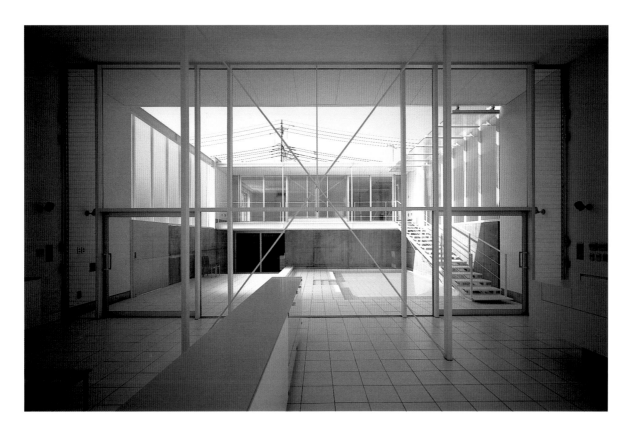

# House in Sakai
Osaka 2001–02

The courtyard within inside (private) and outside (public) concept. This house has two types of courtyard. The one on the west, the most typical in my architecture, planted with greens, assumes a private space for outdoor family activities. Meanwhile, the east courtyard, being both a front yard and the space for entry, assumes public functions. Even though these two courtyards are exterior spaces, they have some sense of interior intimacy at the same time because the levels of both courtyards are on the same level as the interior space.

I tried to create a new space that connects urban space and private space by employing the styles of Japanese traditional courtyards in addition to adding a new interpretation to *tori-niwa* space.

Axonometric section.

View of the south façade with the wooden entrance of the garage and pedestrian entrance on the right.

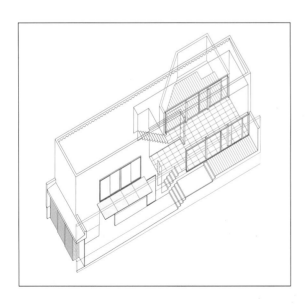

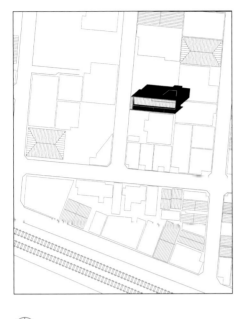

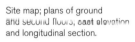

Site map; plans of ground
and second floors, east elevation
and longitudinal section.

Passage along the east front
of the house and views
of the dining/kitchen area.

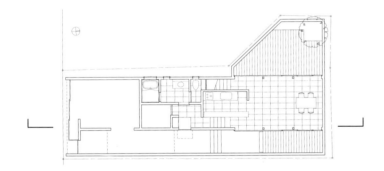

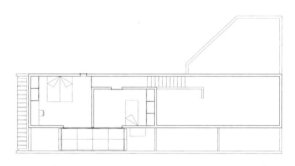

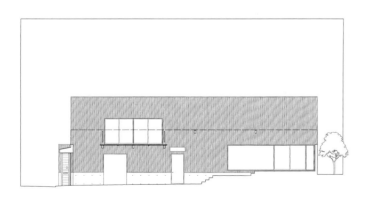

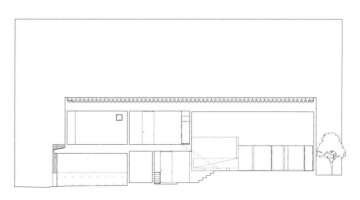

## House in Wakayama
Wakayama 2001–02

The courtyard as forbidden garden. In the *tsubo-niwa* garden of the traditional Japanese townhouse, nature as the extraneous is introduced into the building and domesticated into a microcosm. In the courtyard of this project, I intended to introduce nature in a different way from *tsubo-niwa*. Here we have an abstracted phase of nature, not a microcosm, consisting only of a single tree and a plane of water embodying horizontality. It is a water garden, so we are prohibited from entering the courtyard of the House in Wakayama, in other words, prohibited from entering nature itself.

However, suddenly I realized that the "courtyard one cannot enter" is the very concept embodied in the traditional *tsubo-niwa* courtyard. This, too, is a forbidden garden.

Axonometric projection.

Living/dining area with window on the inner garden.

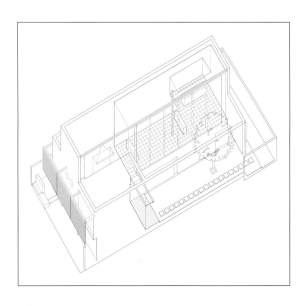

Site map; plans of third, second and ground floors.

Cross section, south elevation and longitudinal section.

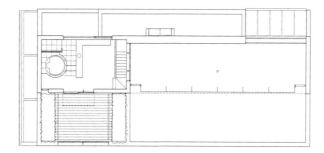

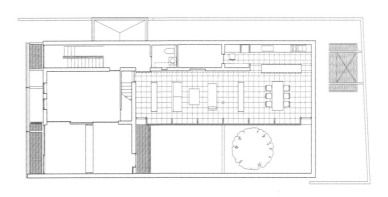

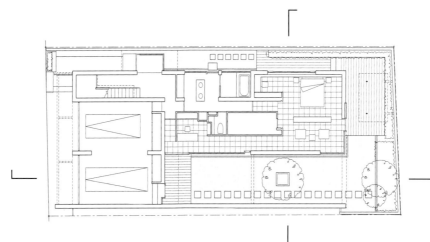

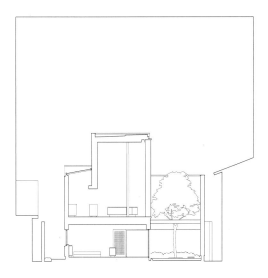

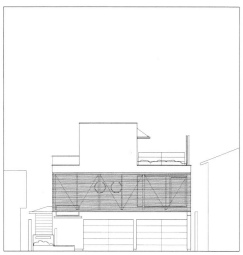

South façade with garage
entrances and views of the garden
with the pool.

View at night of the inner court
with master bedroom at right.

## Hu-tong House
Western Japan 2001–02

This studio-home for a Japanese artist stands out among the two-story one-family homes that surround it by its black metal cladding, which covers the façades and the roof.

The basic idea for the design stems from a visit to southern China, where they have typical courtyard houses called *hakkas*, which are grouped around a network of streets (called *hu-tongs*), used not just as public spaces but as an extension of the space used for certain domestic chores.

The residents extend the concept of *hu-tong* to the internal patio of the home, conceived as a noisy and dynamic space which is comparable to the street rather than a private, silent space.

This "Hu-tong House" is set out as three pavilions linked by an open semi-public passageway. It is conceived as a sequence of spaces that unfold along the path in light-colored wood and never afford a clear overall perception of the building as a whole.

As you approach the house from the main street, the passageway has the function of a vestibule, covered with a lightweight glass roof. On two sides of the central passage are laid out the living quarters, distributed in the pavilions with the need for passages: the bedrooms on the right, the kitchen, dining room and living room on the left. The cross-walls supporting the roof look like the "flats" on a stage and secure the privacy of the various rooms. The third volume that stands at the far end contains a studio laid out on two floors; a small staircase, the final goal of the path begun from the main street, leads to the upper floor and the tatami room.

The whole structure of the complex is made of wood, which, together with the slope of the roofing and plaster ceilings, ensures the sound-proofing required by the owner. With this project, I was seeking a prototype for Asian residential space.

Axonometric projection of the complex.

View from the topmost pavilion towards the shared passage.

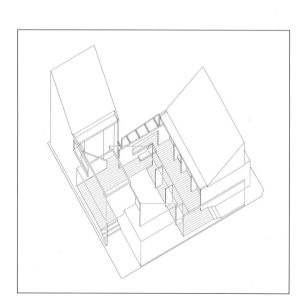

72

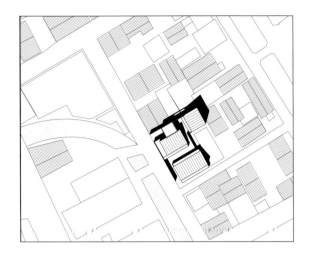

Site map, plans of second
and ground floors.

Sections.

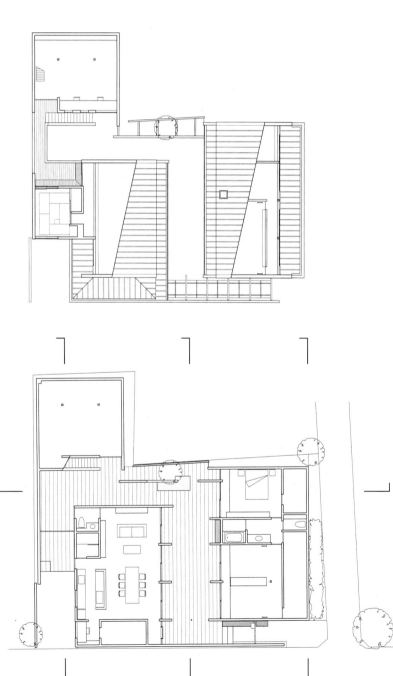

**74**

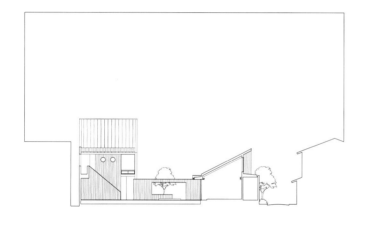

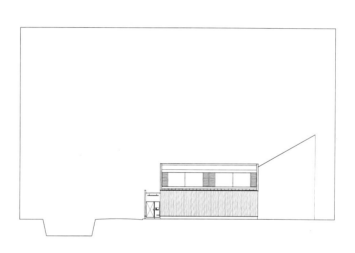

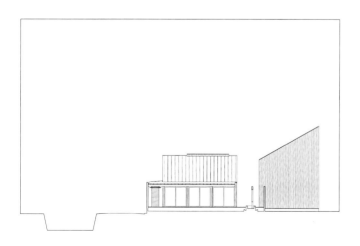

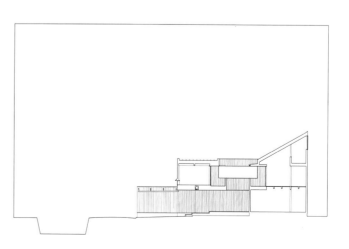

The residential complex seen from above and views of the passage between the pavilions.

The living/dining area and the inner court, showing the walls like the "flats" in a theater separating the rooms.

# House in Higashi-Otsu
Shiga 2001–03

This is a residence for two generations of a family, and consists of several private rooms as well as a living/dining space for all to gather in. Nevertheless, the inner spaces were all designed as white, featureless spaces indifferent to such specific purposes, in an attempt to design the "distance" that the residents would feel within this inner space. The fact that everything inside the building is white already blurs the sense of distance. Moreover, six floor levels and a total of nearly 25 meters of corridors and stairs arranged inside the wooden triple-story structure were intended to bring only the "distance" between the inhabitants to consciousness. By contrast, the living/dining space, which is the final destination of the paths through the house, was planned as a large unified space open to the outside.

The challenge here involved treating the inner spaces as an exterior by adopting a finish that would create the impression that this is the inner space of an architecture to the very end: this meant creating a promenade-like space of white with vague resemblances to some external landscape. For I believe that "interior/exterior" is the most important issue in architecture—the black, matte metal plates used on the exterior finish as opposed to the white interior embodies as well as emphasizes this issue. At the same time, it illustrates my desire that this architecture should draw on the meandering suburban landscape.

Axonometric projection.

View of the east façade.

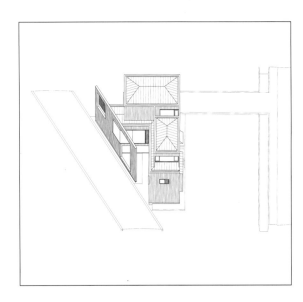

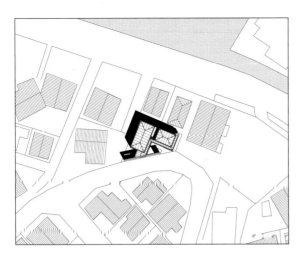

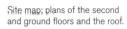
Site map; plans of the second and ground floors and the roof.

South elevation; cross section; detailed section.

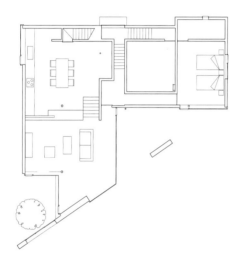

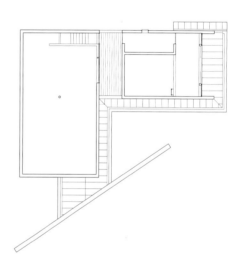

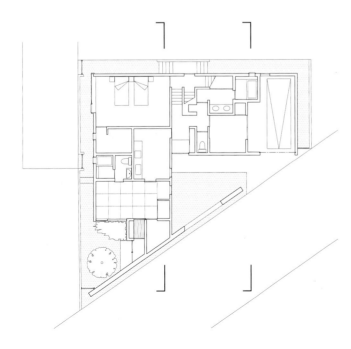

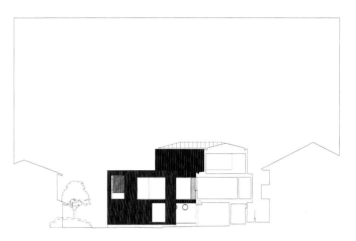

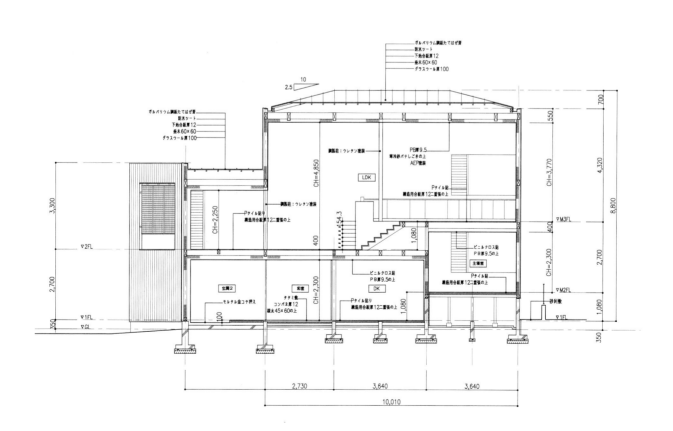

ガルバリウム鋼板たてはぜ葺
防水シート
下地合板厚12
垂木60×60
グラスウール厚100

10
2.5

ガルバリウム鋼板たてはぜ葺
防水シート
下地合板厚12
垂木60×60
グラスウール厚100

鋼製柱：ウレタン塗装

PB厚9.5
寒冷紗パテしごきの上
AEP塗装

700

550

CH=4,850

LDK

Pタイル貼
構造用合板厚12二重張の上

3,300

CH=2,250

鋼製柱：ウレタン塗装

Pタイル貼り
構造用合板厚12二重張の上

54.3

ビニルクロス貼
PB厚9.5の上

主寝室

Pタイル貼
構造用合板厚12二重張の上

CH=3,770

4,320

8,800

▽M3FL

400

400

1,080

▽2FL

2,700

玄関2

モルタル金コテ押え

和室

タタミ敷
コンパネ2厚12
根太45×60の上

CH=2,300

ビニルクロス貼
PB厚9.5の上

DK

Pタイル貼り
構造用合板厚12二重張の上

100

1,080

CH=2,300

2,700

砂利数

▽M2FL

1,080

▽1FL

350

▽GL

350

▽1FL

2,730

3,640

3,640

10,010

Front of the house seen
from the east.

The living room looking towards
the stairs leading up to the
dining/kitchen area; a zone
of the passage and the
dining area.

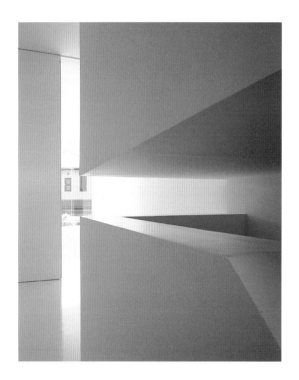

# Residence Annex for K House
Aichi 2002–03

K Residence is a traditional Japanese-style house on a 1,800-square-meter site in a suburban residential district. Despite its ample size and scale as residence, it is a two-story wooden house set low and free in the gentle undulations of the site, with the exquisite alliance between history and contemporaneity found in the modern *sukiya* style.

A small private room was to be planned in the garden. The main building being an example of *sukiya*-style architecture, the importance attached to the garden was greater than usual. Besides, the only corner of the garden where this annex could be placed was inescapably visible from the main parlor. It was then only natural that a structure with floor area less than 100 square meters should be buried under-ground so as to become part of the garden. Embedded in the rich greenery and water of the Japanese garden, only a portion of the wall would show among the green. It would be the image of architecture buried in the garden, like the artificial ruins in English gardens.

Redundancy is inappropriate inside this structure embedded in nature. What we want is not verbose "matter" but just abstracted "texture." And the introduction of "light" to enhance it.

Hence the idea of the overall use of white concrete interfused with limestone powder, cast on-site as exposed concrete. This is concrete white to the core, not painted on the surface. We are now waiting expectantly to see what "texture" will envelop this small building.

Site map of the principal residence with the extension.

Views of the model of the new wing.

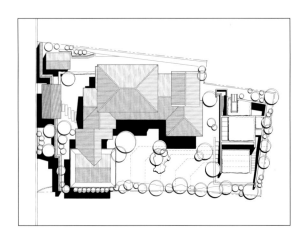

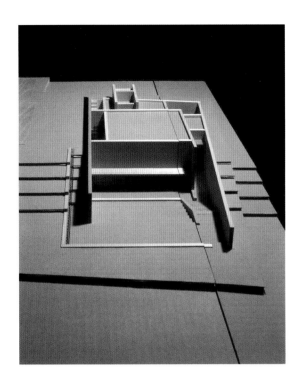

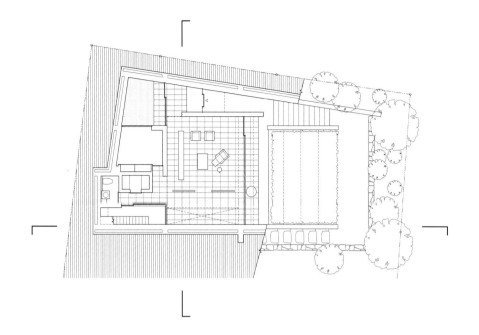

Plan of the ground floor; south
elevation; longitudinal section.

Detailed cross section.

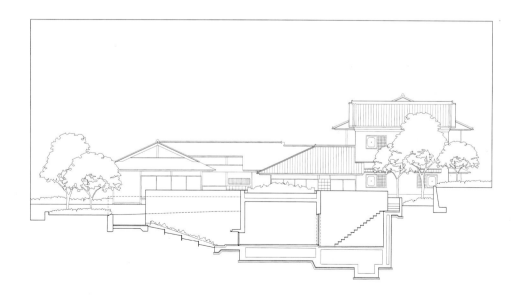

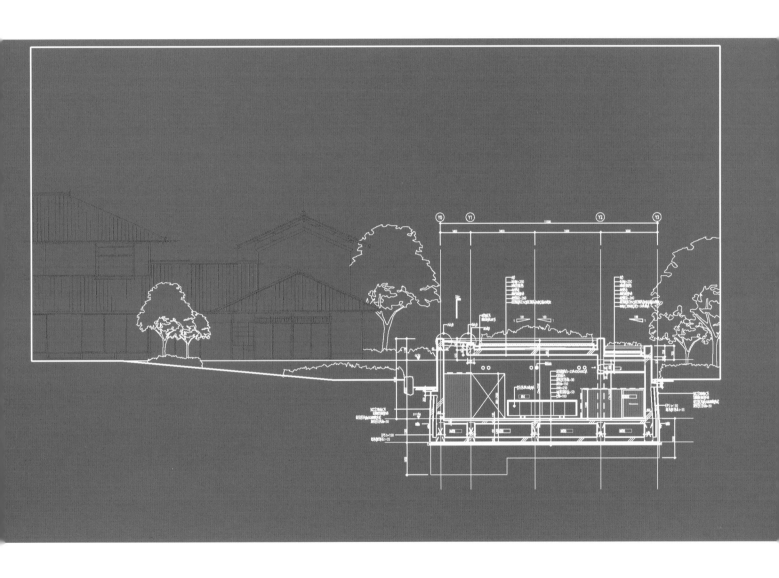

# Standard House 2004
Sakyo, Kyoto 2003–04

My intention here was to create not a one-off "prototype" for a single client, but a house for an imagined, abstract client.

This was to be not a custom-built house but a ready-built house for a specific developer and builder. The small development involved three adjacent lots, each 5.40 meters wide. I decided to use this as an opportunity to develop a standard house for narrow sites.

The first thing I did was to secure the maximum floor area on a site of about 90 square meters. The main volume of the house accommodates bedrooms and storage on the first floor, the living and dining room on the second floor, and a multipurpose Japanese-style room on the third floor. These are connected vertically by a stairway. A washroom, bathroom, toilet and storage are arranged on intermediate levels. Thus the building consists of two volumes of different sizes. A rigid-frame structure of assemblies was adopted for the larger volume. This made possible spaces with a 5.20-meter high ceiling, which is difficult to achieve with ordinary wooden construction. Conventional wooden construction was used for the smaller volume to facilitate any renewal of the mechanical system or additional construction in the future.

Site map.

The third-floor terrace looking towards the dining area.

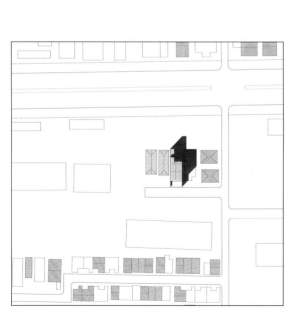

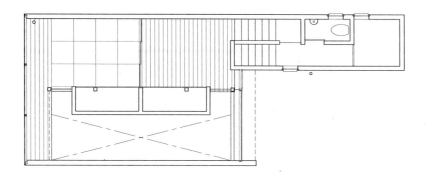

Plan of the third, second
and ground floors.

Longitudinal sections and south
and north elevations.

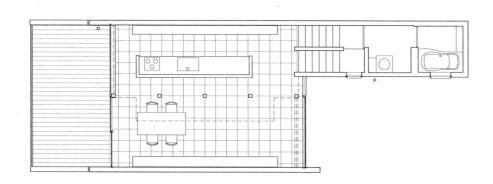

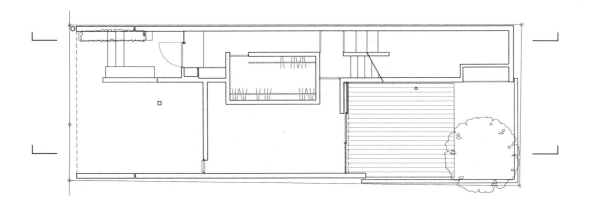

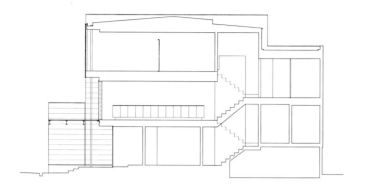

South and north façades.

Views of the traditional Japanese room and third-floor children's bedroom; dining room looking towards the terrace.

# House in Yoyogi-Uehara
Tokyo 2003–

This house for an elderly couple is in a quiet residential district in Tokyo. The ground level is one meter higher than the level of the streets on the west and south sides. There were many regulations concerning the configuration of any building constructed on the site; the overall building form and volume can be said to have been largely determined by those regulations.

The overall organization of the building was deliberately made ambiguous. The building is made up of a number of overlapping volumes, including that of the retaining wall, meaning the site itself. Diverse materials stud the building: they include concrete, glass mosaic tiles, galbarium steel plate, panes of bronzed glass, transparent glass and plaster. Access is from the northwest side, where the difference between the street level and ground level is relatively small. The entry leads directly into the living room. By lowering the floor of the living room below that of the terrace, I was able to give the living room a high ceiling despite the limited overall volume of the building. Basically the interior is one continuous space, but only a fragment of that space is visible at any one time. The interior has been designed as a maze-like space. Although one can hear the voices and sense the presence of the residents from anywhere in this house, they are, as often as not, hidden from view.

Digital model, looking towards the terrace.

Views of the model.

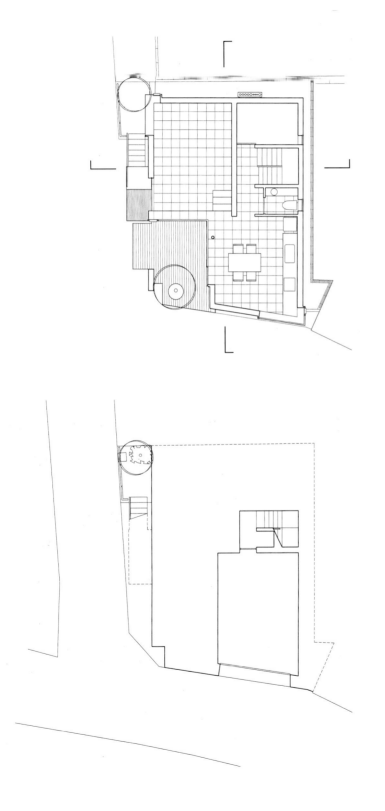
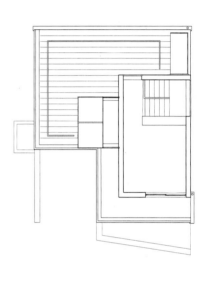
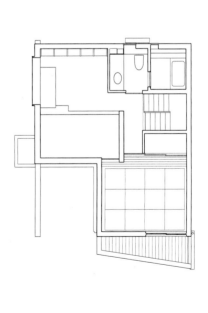

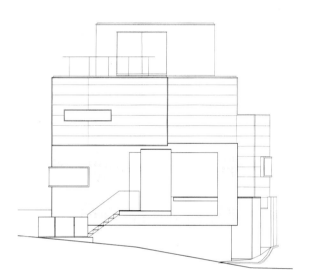

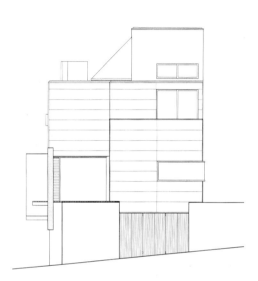

Plans of the ground floor
and basement; the third
and second floors.

West and south elevations;
longitudinal and cross sections.

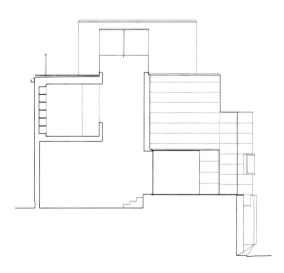

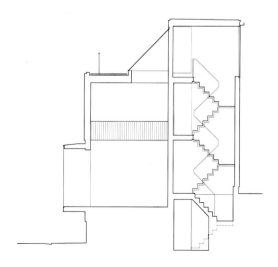

urban projects

## Auto Lab Car Showroom
Ukyo, Kyoto 1989

Standing on a lot on a major road in a Kyoto suburb, this building was designed as a showroom for automobiles. Covered by a 9 × 18-meter roof supported by a steel frame (2 × 4 spans), the showroom forms a single undivided space with a core of sanitary installations. To the east of the building there is a front garden approximately the same size. Customers approach the showroom through the garden, coming from a deck raised 1.20 meters above ground level. Intending to create a diversity of scenery inside the building's simple box and in its surroundings, I used a variety of means to obstruct and, occasionally, blur the view. Examples are the transparent and semitransparent panes of glass fixed directly to the frame with gaskets, the central core which has a certain independence as masonry, the 1.20 meter difference in elevation, the approach which changes direction by 90 degrees several times, and the curved roof which seems to be suspended over the steel frame. At the same time, I attempted to produce a building that is quietly and serenely there—to counterbalance the noise and restlessness not uncommon in today's suburbia.

Exploded axonometric projection.

The exhibition space, looking towards the offices.

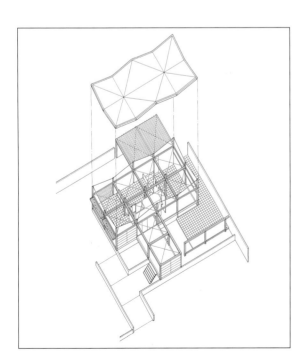

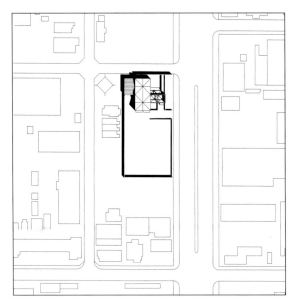

Site map of ground floor
and east-west section.

South front and view
of the external exhibition space.

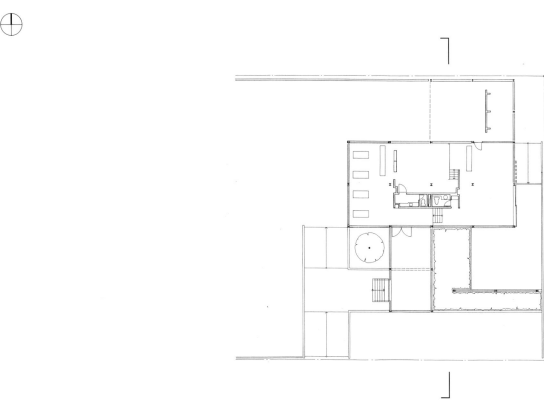

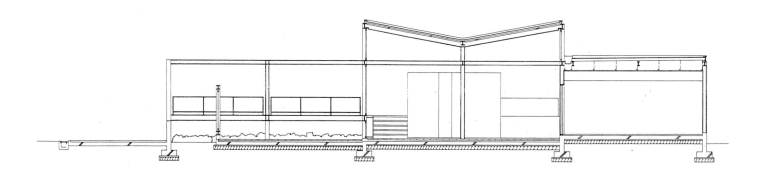

# Kyoto-Kagaku Research Institute

Kizu, Kyoto 1987–90

This building is located in the center of a new business park in Kansai Science City, which is being established in the hills of the Kyoto-Osaka-Nara area. Research conducted in this building centers on the development of restoration and reconstruction techniques for Buddhist statues and excavated cultural treasures. The site is an almost perfectly flat rectangle with a long north-south axis. There is a 3-meter difference in grade between the north and south ends of the site.

I first considered how these natural features might be best used and integrated into my design concept. Eventually I arrived at the solution that can be seen today, in which the main approach to the institute is on the south side and gives access to the building's second floor; a secondary (service and delivery) entrance is provided on the ground floor on the north side. The ground floor, which can also be considered the basement, depending on the observer's point of view, is organized by means of only concrete walls running east to west and north to south, as well as the natural difference in grade. The building was completed by adding a steel-frame construction on top of this ground floor.

The outdoor features—the approach, the terrace on the upper-floor level, the green slope of the front garden, the terraced concrete structure of the outdoor exhibition space, and the central courtyard to the north— are self-sufficient yet at the same time related to one another. On the whole, I placed mutually independent research offices into the expanse and sequence of a varied outdoor space. I chose this concept as I imagined that contact with nature and the seasons would be particularly meaningful to technical specialists whose work on centuries-old Buddhist statues continuously makes them aware of the time gap separating them from the sculptors who created the statues.

Exploded axonometric projection.

Detail of the steel frame
of the north façade.

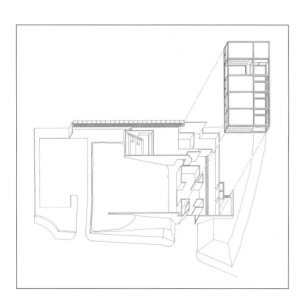

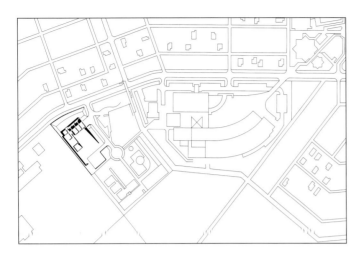

Site map, plans of the second
and ground floors.

East and south elevations
and cross section of the courtyard
in perspective .

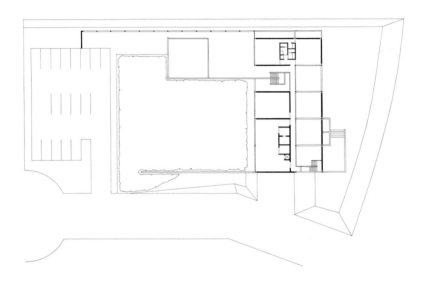

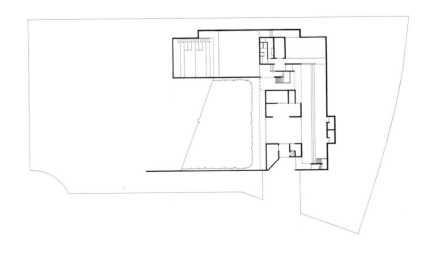

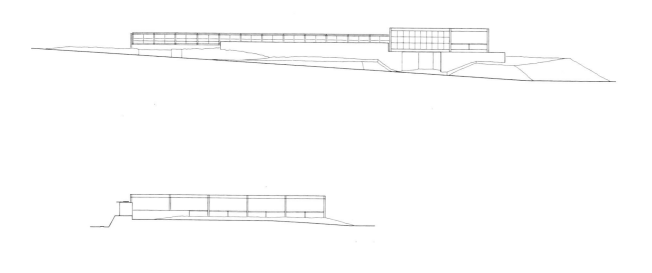

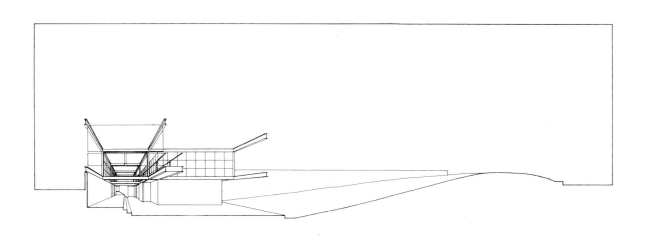

North and east façades.

Views of the transit zones.

External courtyard; views of the internal courtyard.

# Yunoka Footbridge

Ashikita, Kumamoto 1989–91

Yunoura in Ashikita-cho, Kumamoto Prefecture, used to be a popular spa thronged with people who came from Amakusa by ship. Designed as a symbol of the spa's revival, the Yunokabashi footbridge was constructed to replace a wooden red *taiko*-type bridge that had spanned the river of old.

In keeping with its function as a bridge for pedestrians only, it was intended to make crossing the river a delightful experience for its users. To realize this objective, I used a number of technical devices in designing the bridge. First, I decided to provide the bridge with a terrace which would allow people to descend to the surface of the water to relish the immediate sensation of water. Then I employed semitransparent materials for the balustrade. With the sun's rays reflected and refracted by the balustrade, the silhouettes of pedestrians crossing the bridge, I reckoned, would resemble those seen through *shoji* (paper sliding doors). Third, from the very beginning I included illumination effects in my planning, as I also wanted the bridge to be used for pleasurable strolls after nightfall.

Lastly, I based my design on a human scale, not a civil-engineering one, paying particular attention to the architecturally precise detailing of the handrail, as an element directly touched by people's hands. These four basic ideas guided me in the design of the bridge.

Since the bridge was realized, local residents have expressed their enthusiastic approval, to a far greater degree than I had hoped for. This has made me realize—very late, I must admit—an obvious truth: that thinking about bridges also means thinking about people and cities.

Axonometric projection.

The project seen from above.

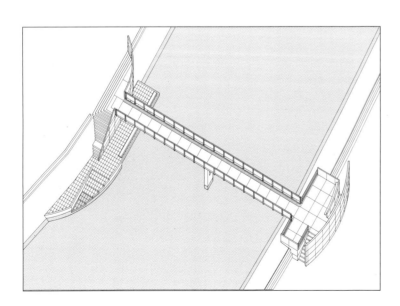

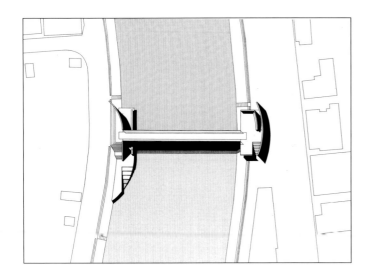

Plan and section in perspective.

Views of the bridge.

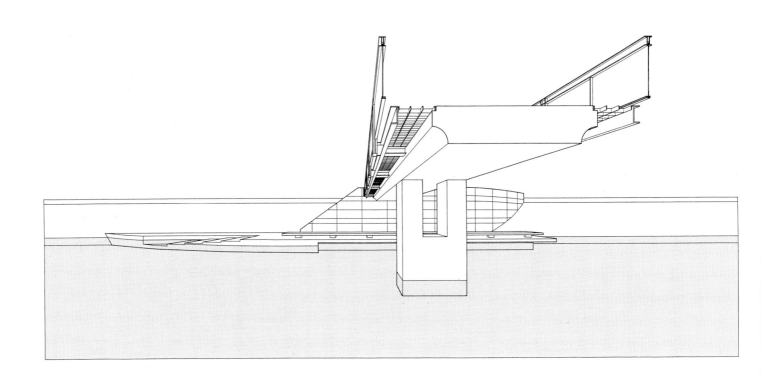

## Sonobe SD Office Building
Sonobe, Kyoto 1991–93

This office building is situated in Sonobe, Kyoto Prefecture, a city with a long and rich history. The center of the city is still pervaded by a nostalgic atmosphere, and it takes no more than a fifteen-minute walk to be among fields and paddies, interspersed with farm houses. The site for the SD office is located in the outskirts of Sonobe, where the urban environment merges into this typically Japanese rural landscape. In planning this project, I had to decide how to interpret the relationship between the surrounding area and the urban context. In other words, what was required of me was an architectural solution to the complex situation of unspoiled nature on the one hand, and the waves of urban erosion on the other.

This means, of course, that particular attention needed to be paid to the planning of the external space. The most appropriate solution was to stress the spatial continuity between the site and its surroundings, and to dramatize the relationship between the internal and external space of the building. The building has three stories—one below ground level, and two above—with most of the total space taken up by an office on ground level with a 7.30-meter high ceiling. The dominant sides of the building are the north and south façades, which run parallel to the streets in front of them. Both sides have glass walls, and a clear-cut north-south axis established between them. Basically, the flow runs parallel to this axis but occasionally intersects it. The overall approach leads from an entirely open space featuring nature to a semi-closed space, and from there to the internal space of the building. This sequence of scenery mirrors the continuous transition from the center of the city to its outskirts. By extending the sequence of scenery to the very interior of the site, the building is firmly positioned in the context of its urban and natural environment.

Axonometric projection.

Detail of the south façade.

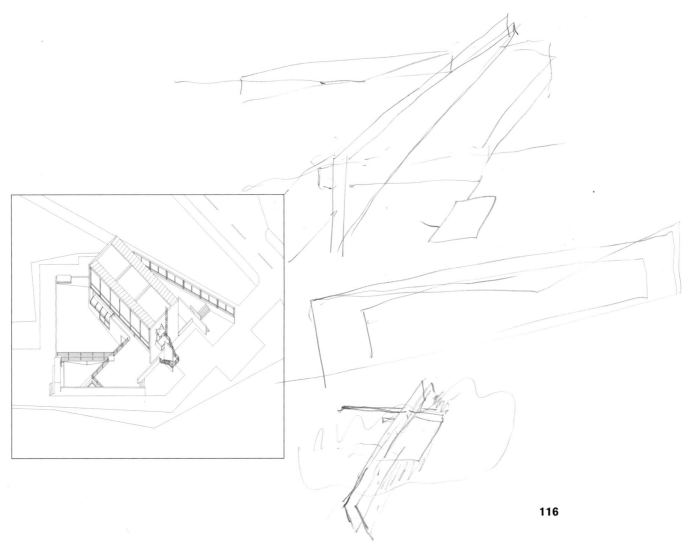

116

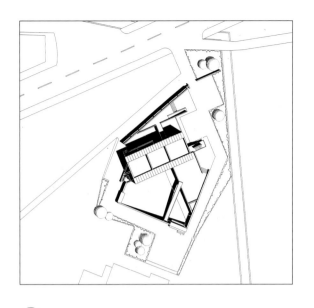

Site map, plans of the basement, ground and second floor.

Southeast elevation, cross section and detailed cross section.

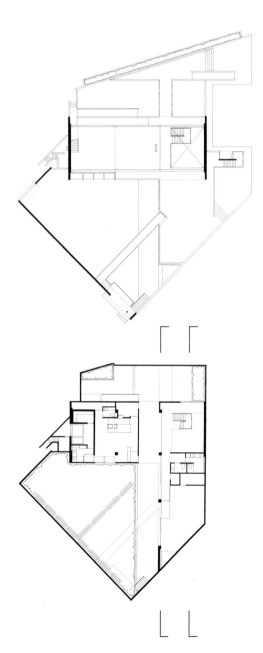

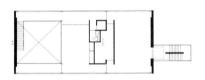

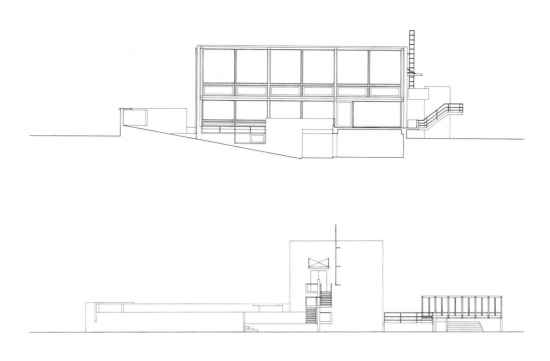

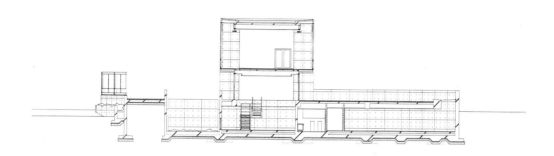

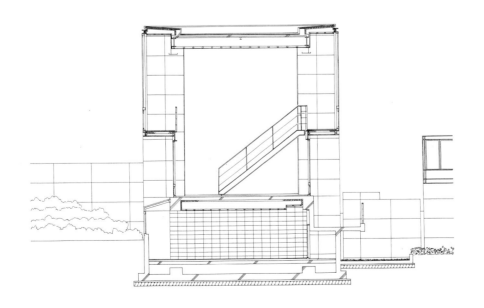

**119**

The terrace and catwalks
to the south entrance.

Interior of the offices.

# Max Mara Headquarters Competition Project
Reggio Emilia 1994–95

The complex consists of five blocks of office buildings and three blocks of common facilities. The site measures about 310,000 square meters, and the building area measures about 31,000 square meters. I thought that the most appropriate solution to the requirements of the brief and the site conditions was to turn the entire site into a park and to treat the building blocks as pavilions. This work provided an opportunity to consider the relationship between the extensive external space of the site and the interior spaces of buildings. It also gave me a chance to reflect on the relationship between architecture and nature. These became the themes of the design.

In traditional Japanese architecture, nature and man exist in harmony. Man is enveloped by nature. In this design, the external space is linked to the internal space of the buildings by means of transitional spaces. The entire site has a park-like character, and the transition from external space to internal space is achieved architecturally through the use of internal courts and terraces.

The concept of light is also inspired by traditional Japanese residential architecture. This is evident in the placing of green areas and inner courts on the north side, and the use of louvers on the south side to cut down glare.

All the structures are a mixture of steel post-and-beam construction and reinforced concrete load-bearing walls. Within the steel frame, outer walls are made of industrially produced prefabricated materials such as precast-concrete panels and steel panels. The reinforced concrete walls are finished in brick —the traditional material commonly used in northern Italy. The brick walls serve as an orienting device on the first floor. Since brick is usually handcrafted, it has something of the warmth of the hand that made it. It is not a uniform material. The brick walls on the first floor can be touched and endow the architecture with a human scale.

A work of architecture is created from the representative materials of an age. It is also affected by the conditions of the site and also closely connected with cultural traditions and the cultural heritage. Steel, glass and cement are materials of the twentieth century, whereas brick is a traditional material. These materials and technologies coexist in the structures of this project. The presence of traditional and modern materials is emphasized. These materials effect a continuity between past, present and future. This design reflects certain aspects of the twentieth century, the cultural tradition and milieu of northern Italy, and the spatial concepts of Japanese architecture.

Site map of the whole complex.

Digital model of parts of the complex built using a mixed system with a steel frame and load-bearing walls made of reinforced concrete and faced with brick.

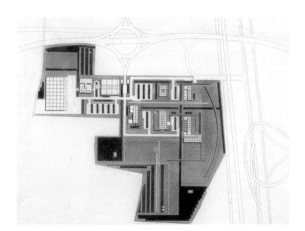

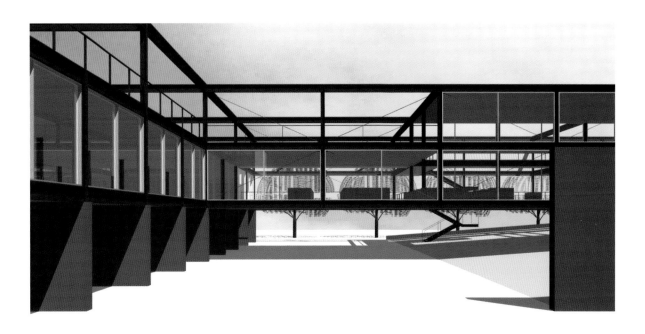

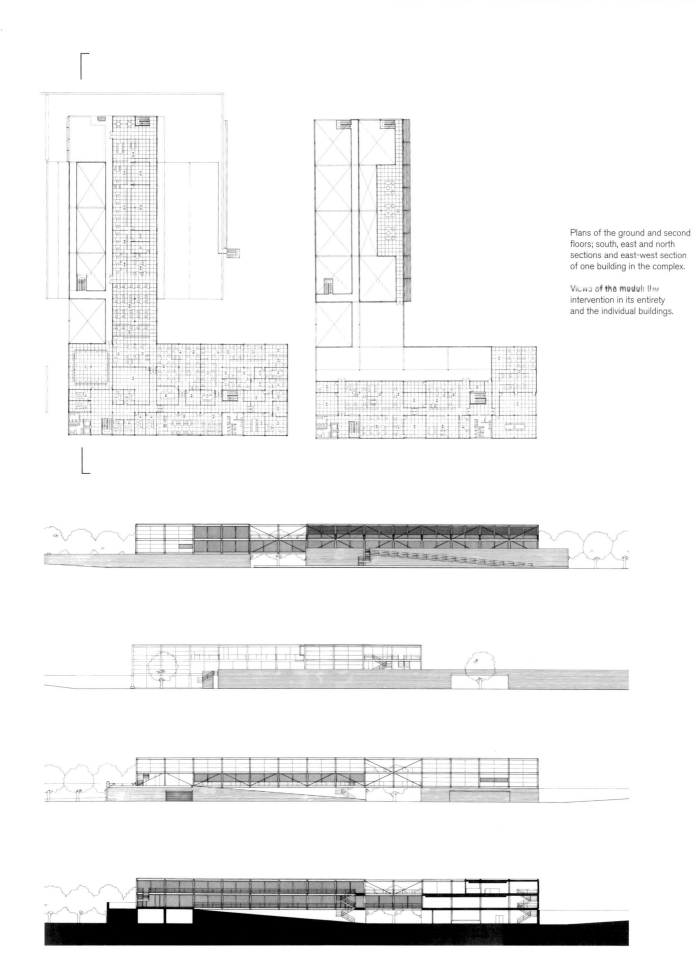

Plans of the ground and second
floors; south, east and north
sections and east-west section
of one building in the complex.

Views of the moduli the
intervention in its entirety
and the individual buildings.

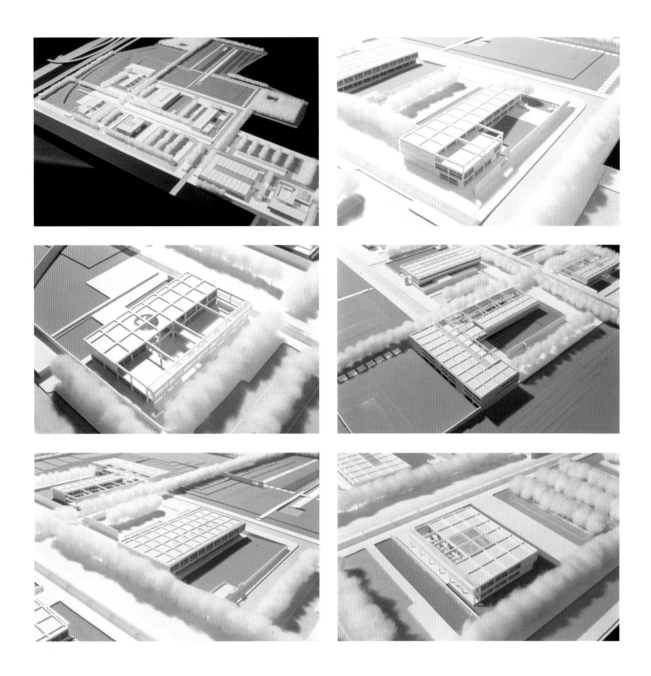

# Murasakino Wakuden Restaurant

Kita, Kyoto 1994–95

This building houses a restaurant serving Japanese cuisine, or more correctly, a shop serving lunch boxes. It is a three-story structure. The first floor is the reception and sales area, where the take-out lunch boxes are sold. The second floor is the main dining hall, and the kitchen and service area are on the third floor. The site has an area of less than 60 square meters. It is bounded on the south side by Kitaoji Avenue, a major thoroughfare that is very noisy. On the west side is a 6-meter wide road, and further west is the Daitokuji temple complex. In this design, a small garden serving as the entrance court was created on the north side. The first floor has an earthen finish and is a quiet space with a closed character. It is in marked contrast to the second floor space which is open to the west. Louvers are used to direct the eye, not to the ground or the sky, but to the greenery of the sprawling Daitokuji complex on the other side of the street. The second floor space is open in character and faces a garden court to the north and the Daitokuji complex to the west. On the first floor, light filters in only through the north court, but the second floor space is full of light. This court is key to the spatial transition in this work. It was a major theme of the design.

A second theme was the question of *Wafu*. How is a Japanese sense of style to be expressed in a reinforced concrete structure? To put it another way, how is the powerful presence of the Daitokuji complex to be acknowledged? The garden court to the north was my solution to these questions. It provides a means of borrowing the verdant scenery of Daitokuji temple complex and creating continuity between the complex and the site. With a road intervening between the site and the complex, it was important to maintain a continuity of greenery. The roof is another way in which a Japanese style has been evoked. Instead of adopting the usual gabled roof, I have shown only the floating edge of the roof. This enhances the importance of the wall and serves to emphasize the exposed concrete wall and the horizontal chestnut panels. These were the means employed to suggest a Japanese style and to acknowledge the presence of the Daitokuji temple complex.

Axonometric projection.

Sales space on the ground floor.

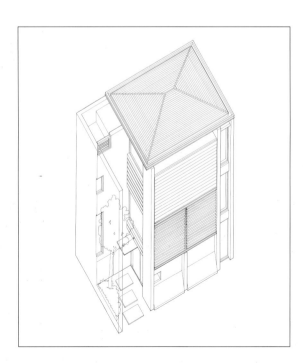

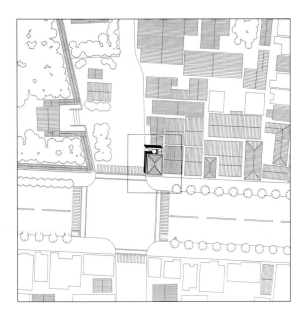

Site map, plans of the second,
ground and third floors;
north-south section.

View of south façade
and west elevation.

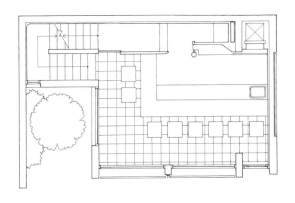

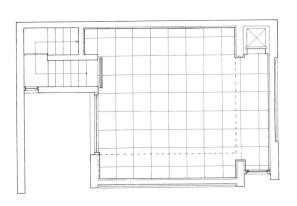

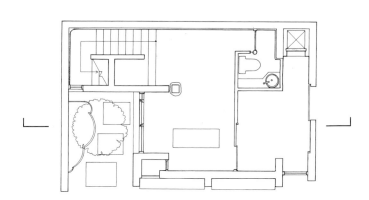

Detail of the west façade.

Views of the restaurant room with the louvers used to guide the eye to the vegetation of the Daitokuji temple complex.

# Competition Project for the National Library Kansai Division

Sieka, Kyoto 1996

When we think of a book we are faced with a paradox. A book is essentially information—and information is without form—yet that information is inscribed on sheets of paper bound together. And perhaps, because of this paradox, books are more than just information. Their material existence sustains fields such as culture and history. The modern library reflects the book's paradoxical character. It is not easy to define the program for a library. In this competition for the National Library in Kansai, the required function is also paradoxical. It is to store books and to transmit formless information. We thus must deal with both visible books and invisible information. We must also deal with the people involved in the library. It was our task to discover how the movements of books, information and people could intersect and to translate our discovery into architecture.

In our proposal, we have a closed mass for the storage and protection of books, and an open volume for the information center. These are both 162 meters long. Between the two volumes is the reading/circulation space, which has a ceiling 30 meters high. This space has, on one side, a view of the bookshelves floating in the shadows within the storage/preservation block, and on the other side, a view of the information center floating in the north light. The movements of books, people and information crisscross and are made manifest in the enormous atrium in the reading/circulation space. The storage block on the south side is completely closed. By contrast, the information center on the north side is open to nature; it has a roof garden and three-dimensionally arranged greenery inside its outer membrane of glass and wood louvers. The reading/circulation room not only mediates

between these two contrasting spaces but is a space flooded with light introduced through the translucent glass on the walls and the roof. This light is an abstract form of nature, and it illuminates by contrast the artificial character of the movements of books, information and people.

The new city in which this site is located has as yet no clear identity. The proposal is a simple form that is intended to stand in marked contrast to the sprawling landscape. The building is situated in the southern part of the site so that an observer looking north from the information center is provided with a sense of depth, namely foreground, middle ground and background. Water has been arranged around the building as a metaphor for nature and suggests to the visitor approaching the facility the contrast between nature and information that is a basic concept of this design.

Digital model of the transitional room between the two main volumes.

Views of the model.

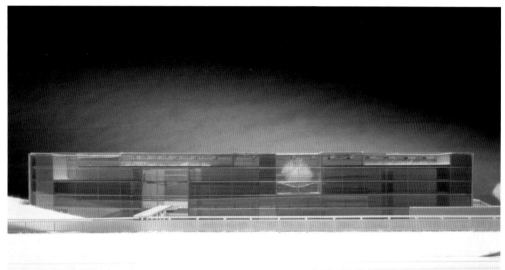

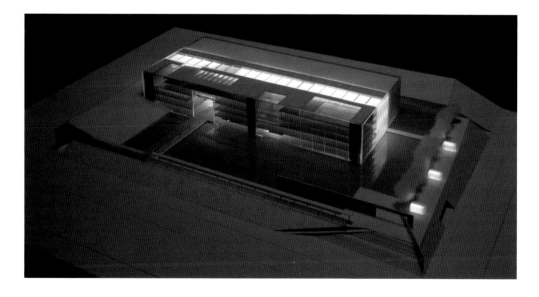

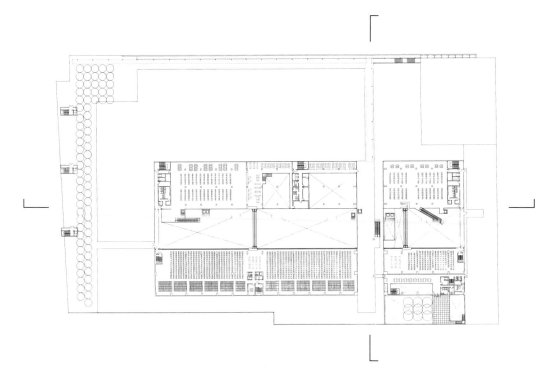

Plan of the ground floor, longitudinal and cross sections and west elevation.

Digital model of the complex surrounded by the water and view of the circulation zone between the buildings.

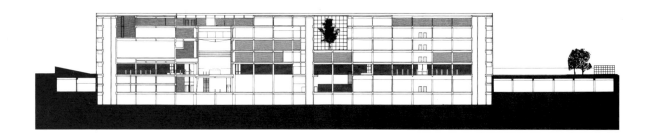

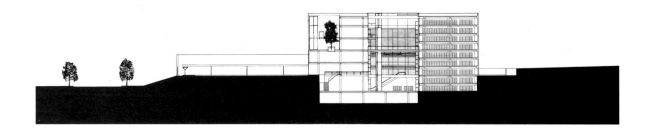

# Yamaguchi Memorial Hall

Ube, Yamaguchi 1994–97

This building is for the medical faculty of Yamaguchi University. It commemorates the 50th anniversary of the institution and was donated by the alumni association. Although it is an alumni hall, it is a place not just for alumni reunions but also for the discussion of cutting-edge themes in the field of medicine. It houses facilities for conferences, meetings, research seminars and lectures. Students, faculty and employees of the university can also come here to relax. The hall is located in a garden that was donated earlier by supporters of the university and that has long been frequented by students and the university staff. Thus, the place already possessed a significant reality and was associated with many fond memories. The new building was an attempt to reinforce rather than to erase that reality or those memories. The design is intended to integrate the architecture and the garden and to produce a new place in the campus. The old memories have not been erased but woven into a new landscape. The layering of old memories and a new structure creates a sense of place and ultimately a sense of history within the campus.

The main approach to the hall is over a pond in the Japanese garden. The path then turns 90 degrees to the right. The western third of the building is an outdoor terrace that leads to the first-floor entrance hall and a ramp.

Most of the spaces, with the exception of the top-floor conference room, face the garden or the abundant greenery in the campus. For a brief moment, people are able to forget the stresses of being in a medical school.

Axonometric projection.

View looking towards the entrance footbridge.

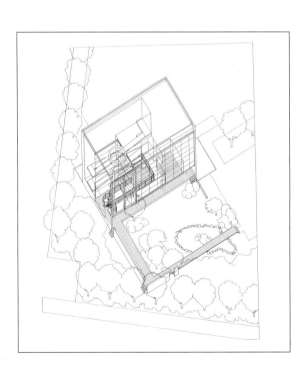

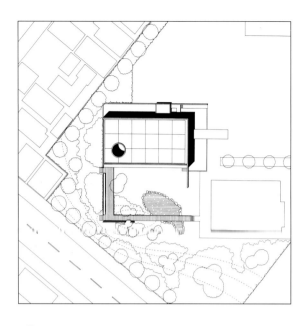

Site map, plan of the ground,
third and second floors.

Longitudinal and cross sections.

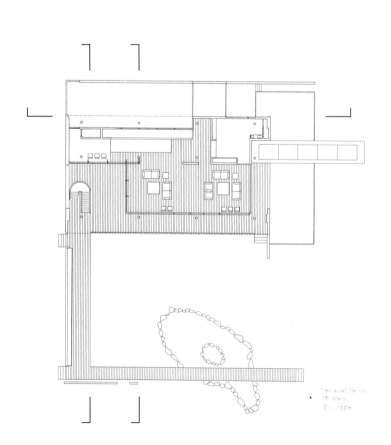

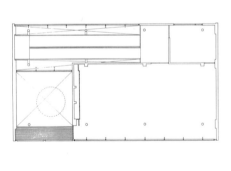

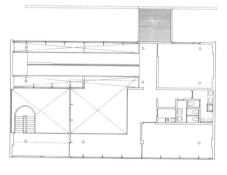

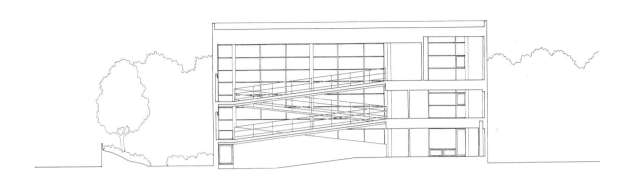

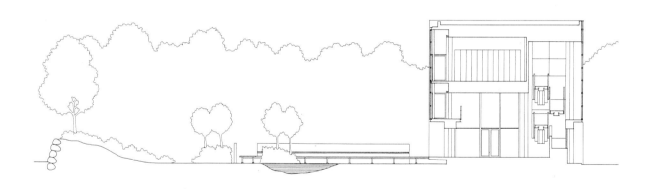

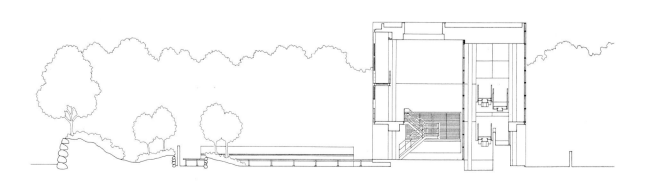

**139**

South façade and view
of the footbridge giving access
to the building.

Views of the interiors.

## Kazurasei Antique Gallery
Nagayo, Kyoto 1998–2000

This antique gallery is located southeast of Kyoto's Imperial Palace on Teramachi-dori, an avenue lined with venerable shrines and antique shops. The site is deep with a narrow frontage, a kind of building site that is typical of Kyoto. On this site I placed a three-level volume.

Pivotal to the design are two voids inserted vertically in the center of the volume—a court and a skylight. The court, with light spilling silently from above on a composition of water and stone, is almost a light court. The skylight, by contrast, is an internal space with a staircase that rises through uniform light filtered by *shoji* screens.

The court with its abstract composition and concrete materials, and the skylight with its tranquil light and the movement implicit in its stairs: By placing these elements in confrontation in the center of the building, I sought to orchestrate the transition of spaces from the ground-level gallery to the second level. I was pursuing a building which, despite the blank expression of its façade, would contain a quality of internal space that would be somehow excessive. This gallery is the result.

Axonometric projection.

The east façade with entrance to the exhibition spaces at right.

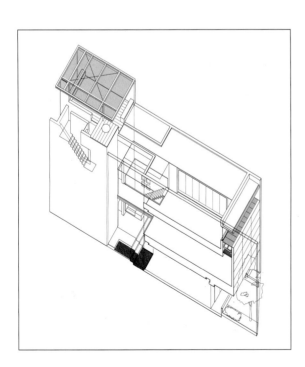

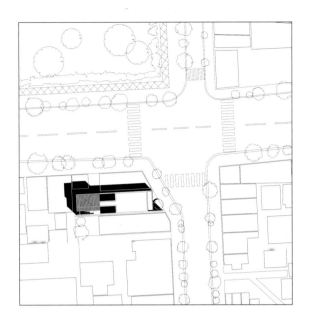

Site map; plans of the second and ground floors, of the roof and third floor.

South elevation and longitudinal and cross sections.

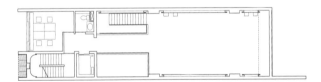

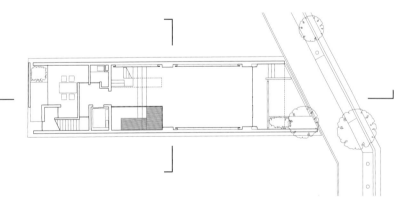

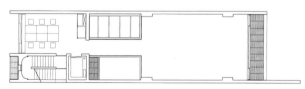

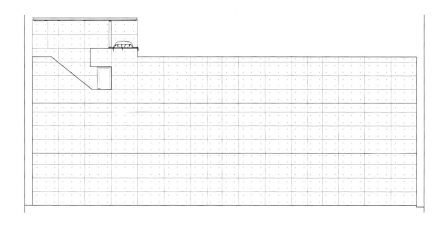

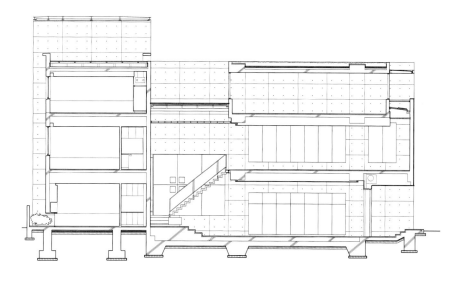

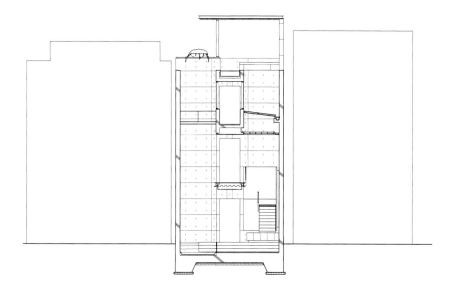

Exhibition rooms on the ground and upper floor.

View of the ground-floor living room looking towards the main entrance and the internal stairs.

# Urban Project of the Teresitas Beachfront
Santa Cruz de Tenerife, Canary Islands 2000

The site is composed of two distinct landforms, separated by a low hill. On the ocean side is a bluff rising from the shore, in a landscape of color bands: the blue of the ocean, the white of the beach, the green of the verdant slope. Towards the mountain is an alluvial fan at the foot of the mountain: a horizontal expanse of land opening toward the ocean.

I proposed to give each landform its own architectural form so as to merge the architecture with the site. On the ocean side is placed a layered volume, terraced with the slope so as to appear immersed in the lush green landscape. On the side towards the mountain are stepped water plazas with interlocking surfaces, designed for optimum harmony with the flat expanse below the mountain. Common to these contrasting architectural forms is a sense of integration, rather than confrontation, between inner and outer spaces, and between the architecture and the verdant nature encompassing it. On the ocean side, the architecture is unified with the green slope; while on the side towards the mountain, stepped water plazas give architectural articulation to the natural landform.

The crux of my proposal is architecture that will merge with the landscape through its encounter with greenery and water.

General view of the model.

Site map of the project.

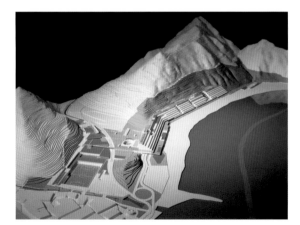

**149**

Front of the complex from
the sea and the city; longitudinal
and cross sections.

Digital model of the complex
towards the south and one
of the internal public spaces.

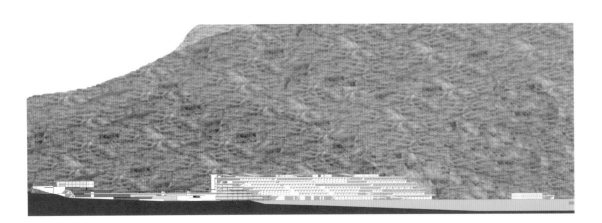

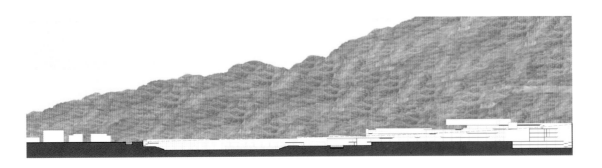

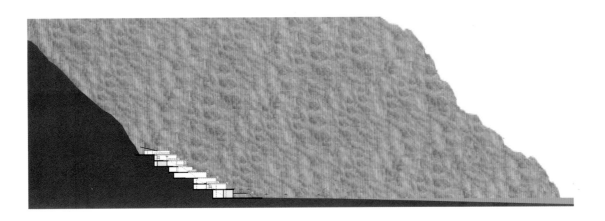

## Stadium 600 Pachinko Arcade
Nagoya, Aichi 2000–01

This is a 470-seat pachinko gaming hall in a commercial area near the center of Nagoya. In part because of their flashy exteriors, suburban pachinko halls have attracted a great deal of attention in recent years, but this project involved the rebuilding of an existing facility in the middle of the city. Although there is a narrow street at the back, this is essentially an urban building with just a single façade. In such cases, the standard solution has been to make the façade of the pachinko hall as eye-catching as possible. However, the nature of the pachinko business and the environment in which the business operates have been changing lately. The image projected by pachinko halls has also been undergoing change. I came to the conclusion that an approach completely opposite from the conventional one might be taken in such an urban environment. I decided on a quiet scheme seeming at first glance to blend into the townscape was possible.

The internal spaces of a pachinko hall must be cut off completely from the outside world. Time as experienced inside the hall has no relation to real time. It is irrelevant whether it is day or night outside the building. It is precisely to escape the—everyday flow of time that people frequent pachinko halls. A pachinko hall is not unlike a theater or a cinema in that respect. I decided to compose the façade in such a way that passersby could not see anything inside at eye level but could sense something of the atmosphere inside from openings on a higher level, meaning a sort of piano nobile. The building is composed of three spatial layers arranged parallel to the street. First, there is a high-ceilinged, shallow but wide entrance hall, in which the clamor of the street still seems to linger. Second, there is the space of the actual pachinko hall, which is like a theater during intermission, because it suggests human presence even when empty. Third, there is the rear

entrance hall, a space that is like a theater foyer where the excitement of the audience is allowed to subside after a play has ended.

These three spaces and the fourth, outside space of the city at large are not connected but divided into separate parts, so that one experiences the building as one does a four-act play.

I must admit that while I was designing this work I thought of the spatial organization of the Teatro Olimpico and the Kanamaruza (a late Edo-period Kabuki theater in Kotohira, Kagawa Prefecture). I wanted to see if a building could not be made into a theaterlike spatial collage. Unlike my previous works, this building is not designed in the manner of a motion picture, meaning as a sequence of scenes. I felt that such an approach was not conducive to the creation of a theater-like space suggestive of an accumulation of dream fragments. On the contrary, it was necessary to cut the sequence into distinct parts.

South façade.

View of the gaming room.

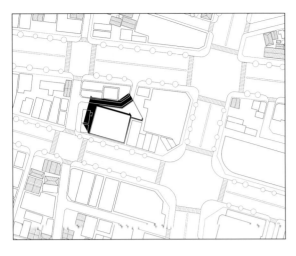

Site map; plans of the ground and second floors: east-west and north-south sections.

View of the staircase leading up to the second floor from the bar.

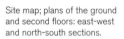

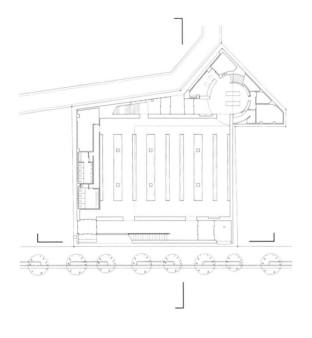

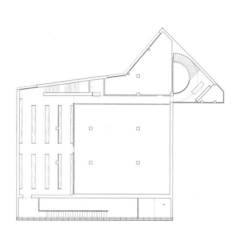

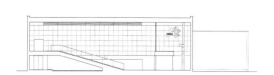

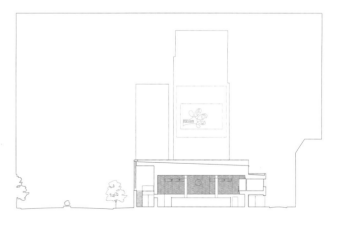

# Competition Entry for the Eda Housing Complex
Yokohama, Kanagawa 2002

This was an entry in the first round of a limited competition for an apartment building.

The site is in a suburb, in front of Eda Station on the Tokyu Den'entoshi Line, about 30 minutes away from the center of Tokyo. Apartment buildings stand in the vicinity of the site. An apartment is not a substitute for a detached house. I wanted to propose an apartment building that would offer a lifestyle not possible with detached houses. The units proposed here are not the usual apartment units with deep, narrow plans and an entrance accessed from a corridor. Two thin blocks, arranged parallel, have been cut out three-dimensionally, and maisonette units have been combined like pieces of a three-dimensional puzzle. Basically, each unit has a private outdoor space such as a double-height terrace or a court.

This proposal for an urban lifestyle provides units that enable residents to live in close contact with nature without always having to go to a park. It also suggests a form of community in a suburb of an enormous city that is possible only in apartment buildings.

Digital model of the interior of a standard apartment with double-height private terrace.

Views of the model.

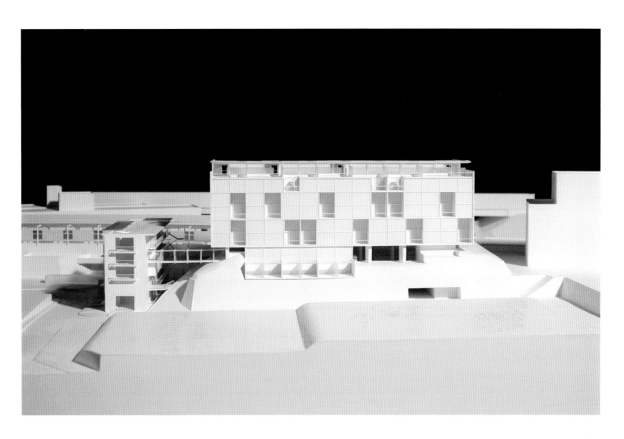

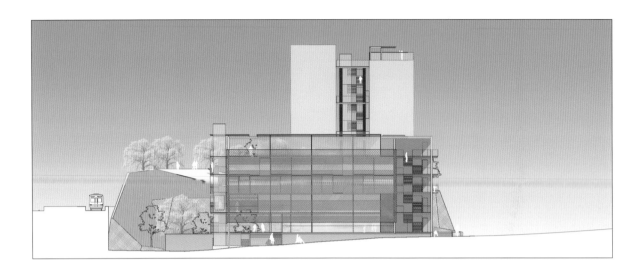

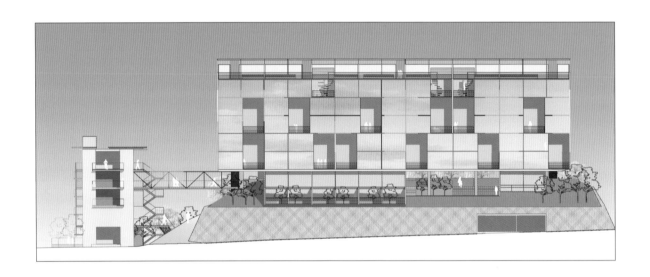

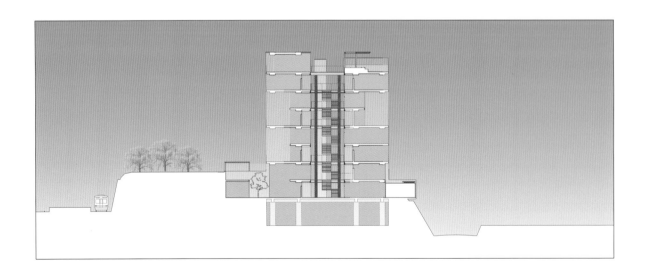

North and west elevations;
cross section.

Digital model of the transit zones
and public areas.

# Competition Project for the Nam June Paik Museum

Kyonggi, South Korea 2003

This was an entry in a competition for an art museum dedicated to an artist who works in video art. The difference between traditional art and video art is that video art is not itself a material medium. It can be said to have no physical character. A museum dedicated to such an art should not be based on a conventional concept of architecture. A building for the display of works that question the conventional definition of art—and of course "work" is itself a problematic concept in this context—should not be acquiescent. That was the starting point for this project.

I felt that Nam June Paik should be regarded not as an artist but as an activity. What was needed here was not a building to accommodate works but a site for such activity.
I proposed only a place, namely a horizontal floor excavated and distinguished from the landscape, like the sites at Ellora and Ajanta, and covering that entire place an irregularly-shaped roof that almost mimics a landscape.
Here it is not the architecture but the place that is defined by the roof, which in effect creates a site where activity occurs.

Digital model of the interior of the museum spaces.

Views of the model with the topography of the site, roof and layout of the interiors.

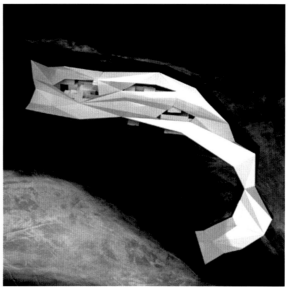

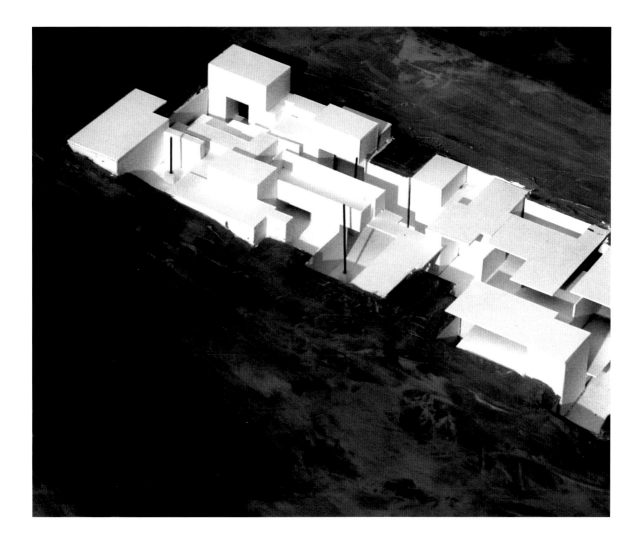

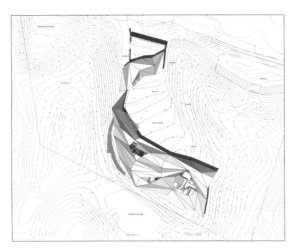

Site map of the project; plans
of the building on the upper,
intermediate and lower floors.

North and west elevations,
cross and longitudinal sections.

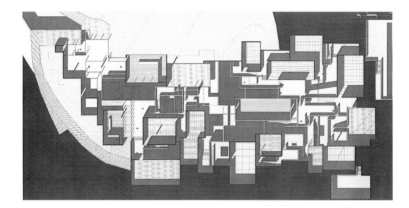

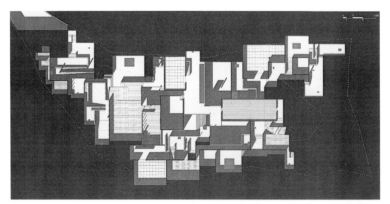

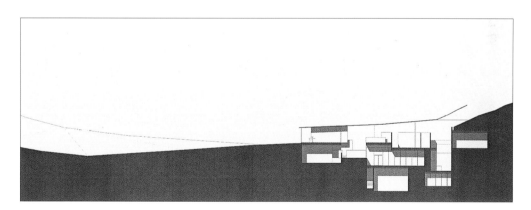

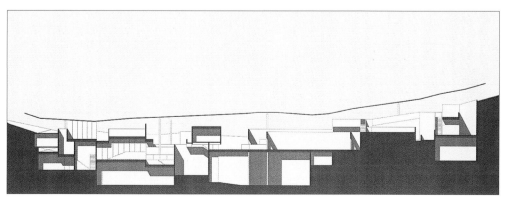

## Meridian Line Akashi Ferry Terminal
Akashi, Hyogo 2002–03

This building is a terminal for a ferry line linking Awaji Island to the mainland. Functionally, it is quite simple and consists of two spaces: A waiting hall with a ticket counter and toilets and a passageway leading to the gate where tickets are presented before boarding.

The waiting hall is the main space in this building. I tried to give spatial expression to certain images the client had suggested at the start of work on the design: Akashi (a scenic coastal area in the region with ancient literary associations), the meridian (135° E, used for Japanese Standard Time) and an astronomical observatory. The building is a simple, closed box with two types of openings. One is a cruciform opening in the ceiling that is off the building's axis but aligned with the true north-south axis. The light entering through the opening not only serves as a sun dial but together with the slightly domed configuration of the ceiling is

meant to highlight the fact that this place stands on a meridian. I also made the ceiling domed so that the light falling on the floor or wall would be distorted and not form a perfect cross; I wanted the light simply to serve as a sun dial and not take too symbolic a form. To emphasize the narrow opening, I made the roof structure a monocoque of steel plate, reinforced only where necessary with steel members. The resulting roof plate is basically cantilevered; columns are erected only where they are structurally required. The building is a type of camera obscura, projecting an image representing the world outside. If a journey is a process of confirmation for oneself of what exists in the outside world, then entering the waiting hall, where one encounters an image of the world, can be said to be the first step in that process.

The other opening in this space is a long, horizontal bay window. Its

form was determined after repeated studies to make certain it would introduce no light that might weaken the effect of the light from the ceiling and would frame a view only in the direction of the impending journey, only toward the sea. I wanted this picture window to frame the world in a different way from the opening in the ceiling.

The passageway, the other space of the terminal, is completely different from the waiting hall by being a space of reality. I wanted to create a blunt, matter-of-fact space by using nothing but familiar, ready-made industrial products such as the window of aluminum louvers and figured glass (installed in an exposed frame of section steel) and the tent roof. Once they have gone through the enclosed space of the waiting hall, passengers abruptly encounter once more the city of reality and the sea on which they are about to set sail.

Site map of the complex.

View of the waiting lounge with the cross-shaped skylight in the roof.

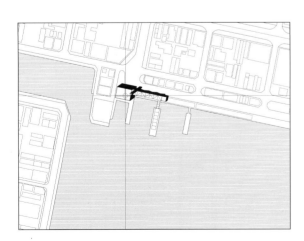

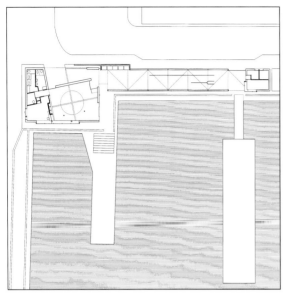

Plan of ground floor; north and
south elevations; cross section.

Detailed cross section
of the waiting room.

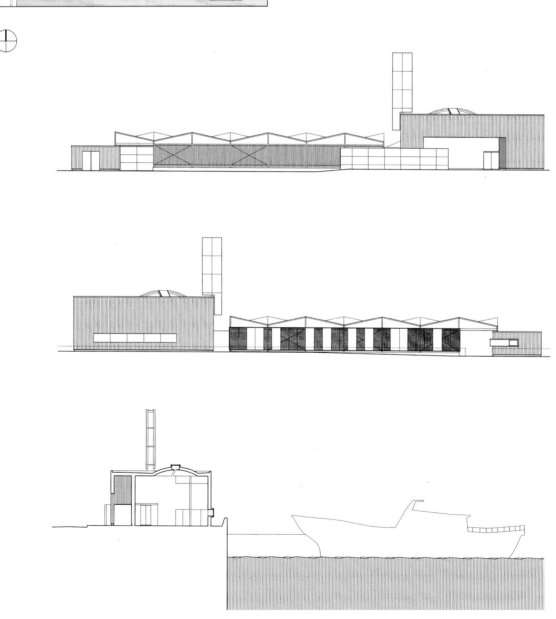

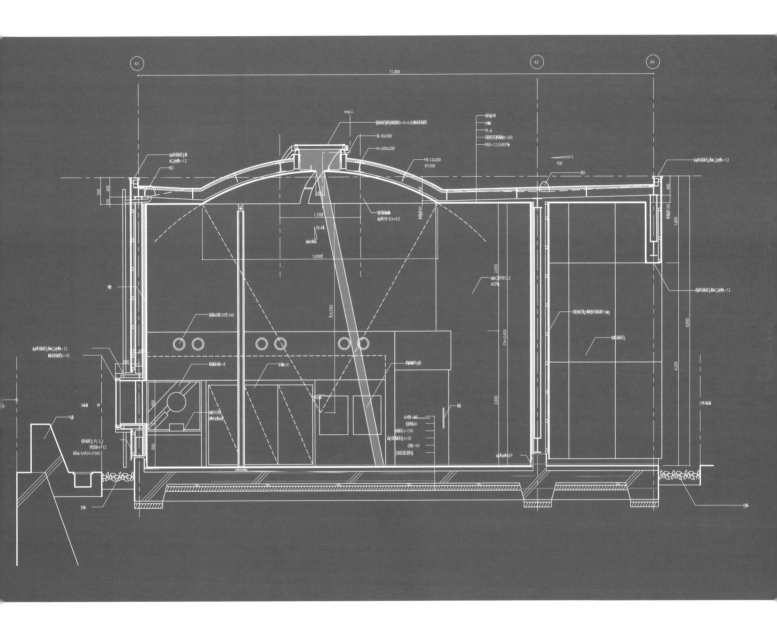

Details of the north elevation
and the façade system.

View of the passage
linking the waiting room
to the departure area.

# Competition Project for the Kumano Forest Information Center
Owase, Mie 2003

This was a competition entry for an information center whose theme was the natural preservation of forests. I once visited Muir Woods, a grove of virgin redwood trees north of San Francisco. I learned then that the very presence of human beings is destructive to a forest. When human beings enter a forest, they introduce new light and air into that forest. This alters the forest ecology and destroys nature. Light and wind, which we normally consider a part of nature, can prove destructive to the natural environment of a virgin forest. It was made painfully clear to me that there is no one, correct definition of nature.

In this case, I wanted to create a space that would enable visitors to sense the reality, meaning and character of nature in a virgin forest. A road is a form that permits minimal contact between a forest and human beings. By contrast, an outdoor space such as a plaza or a courtyard lets in an abundance of sunlight and permits the free circulation of air. Here I proposed an architecture of forest and road.

The proposed building does not possess architectural elements familiar to us, such as columns and roofs. Timbers made from trees cut near the site are piled up almost casually, and an inner space in the form of a road is cut through them. Inside, there is only the light that has passed though the structure of piled timber. I wanted the experience of this building to be like a walk in the woods. I felt that providing such an experience should be the only function of a forest-related information center.

Diagrams showing the building's response to environmental conditions.

View of the model.

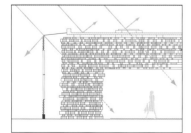
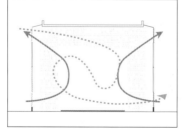
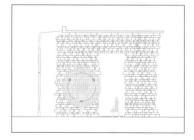

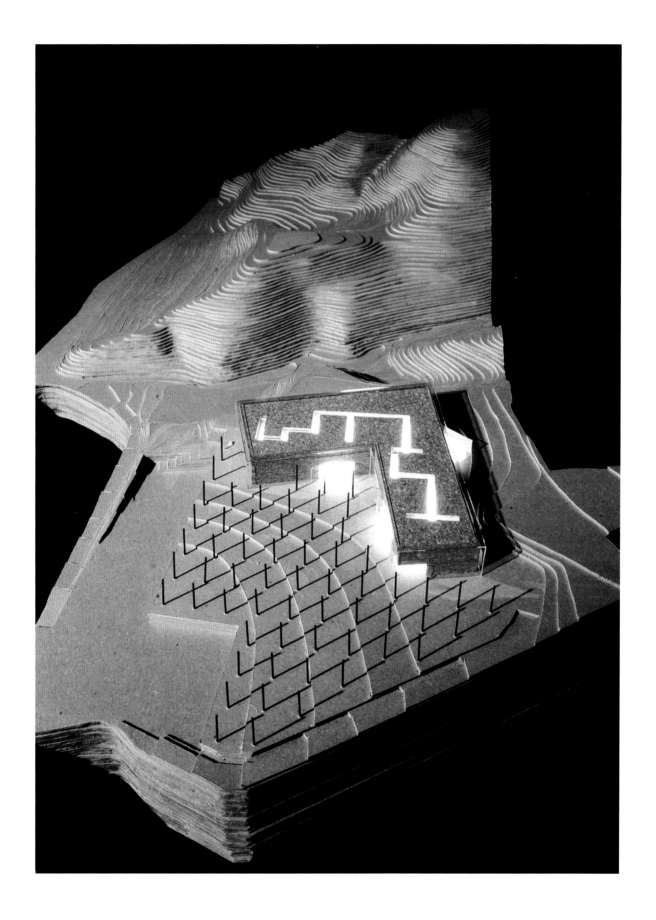

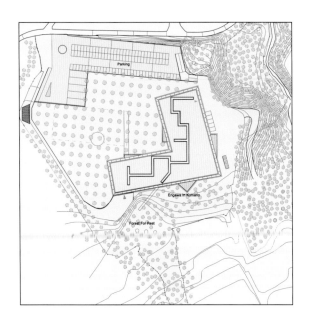

Site map; plan of ground floor; west elevation; section through the service areas.

Digital model of the interior.

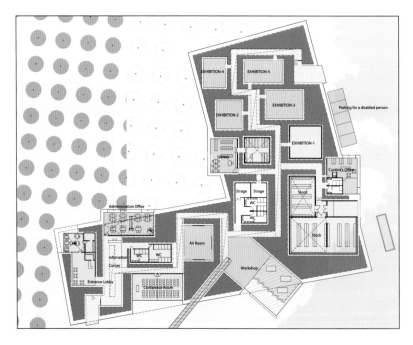

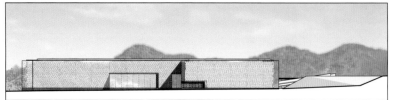

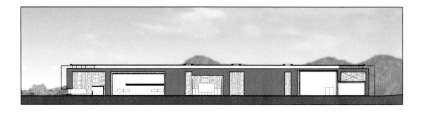

## Sumida Dental Clinic
Amagasaki, Hyogo 2002–04

This clinic is in a suburb of Osaka, in a place where there is still a great deal of farmland.

It is basically a one-story, L-shaped building arranged on a rectangular site completely enclosed by a wall. Between the wall and the building are two outdoor spaces. One is a public courtyard for the clinic, and the other is a private courtyard for the staff. The indoor spaces look out on these courtyards. The public courtyard is paved in black lava rocks and planted with one tree. The wall facing the courtyard is composed of dark-colored wood and white plaster and creates a quite different impression from the silver façade of the building on the outside, which is finished in galbarium steel plate. I wanted visitors to the clinic, who are naturally anxious about their health, to feel at ease the moment they enter the courtyard.

The same wood material and white wall surface are used in the interior space. The space is deliberately displaced from the structure so that the waiting area leads easily and almost imperceptibly to the examination room.

The private courtyard to the north has a wooden deck. An opening in the wall affords a view of the surrounding landscape. This courtyard is open to the outside. I wanted to make this a place where people working in the clinic can feel free and at ease during time off duty.

South elevation.

The complex, looking north.

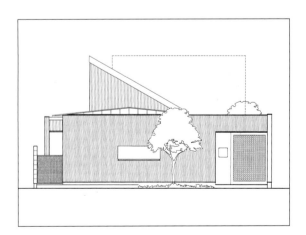

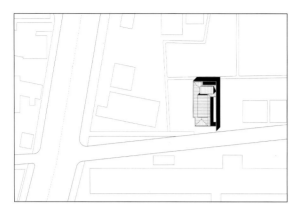

Site map; plan of ground floor;
cross section; longitudinal section.

Views of the court and interiors.

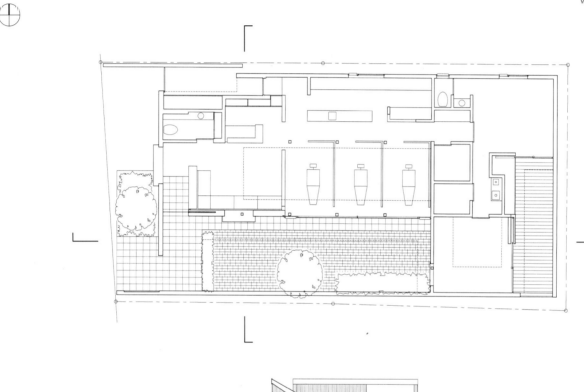

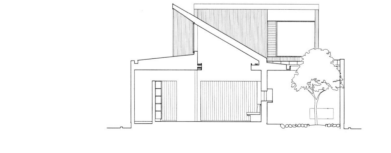

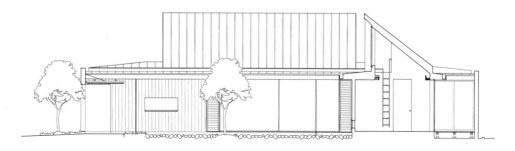

**178**

## Paju SW Office
Seoul, South Korea 2001–04

This project is for an office building in a new research park, currently under planning for a location near an airport, about an hour from central Seoul. The site is in an area of lush greenery, backed by mountains, and has a river running before it.

After reflecting on the best response to such an environment, I decided to use glass of three different kinds of transparency—transparent, frosted, and stripe-print—to screen the interior space from the exterior. Applying these materials enabled me to manipulate the visual relationship between the interior and exterior and to avoid an architecture that imposed itself harshly on the surroundings.

I employed staggered floor levels for the interior spatial composition. By inserting a staircase in a vertical void topped by a skylight and placing a ramp along an exterior glass curtain wall, I connected the floors with a gentle, spiraling path of movement. This open design engenders a perception of the office building's interior as a single space.

View of the model.

North façade.

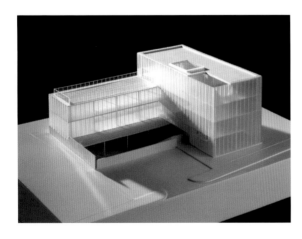

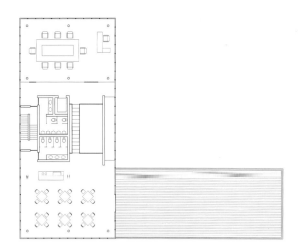

Plans of the third and ground
floors; north-south section.

View of the south façade.

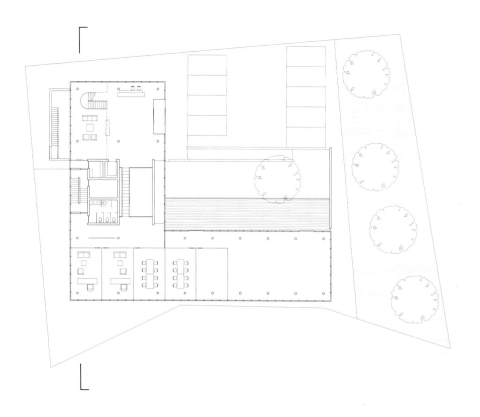

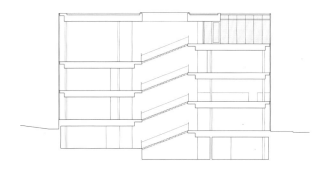

Views of the transit
and linking zones.

# Gifu Kitakata Housing
Gifu 2002–

Arata Isozaki was in charge of the overall planning, and twenty-one teams of architects including my office designed the individual apartment buildings. Isozaki was responsible for the site plan and the overall planning of the apartment buildings. He designed the structural and mechanical systems for the apartment buildings. We architects designed the units in the sectors assigned to us and were in charge of the interior spaces and façades.

The program provided ample space for the units in the assigned sector. That made it possible to create interior spaces and terraces not usually found in apartment buildings, such as deep terraces, double-height spaces, and units that occupy two floors and are not simply sandwiched between walls.

By contrast, I made the overall elevation as simple as possible in composition. The exterior gives no hint of the organizational diversity of the interior spaces. I wanted the organization of the internal spaces and the units to reflect the lifestyles of residents and the outer façade to express the identity of the structure as an apartment building. Eventually, the buildings in this project will become a part of the anonymous city. No one can predict what they will look like in the end. Not even Isozaki, the overall planner, can say what their ultimate appearance will be like. That is in the nature of a city.

Diagrams of the different types of apartments.

Plans of the eight levels of the building.

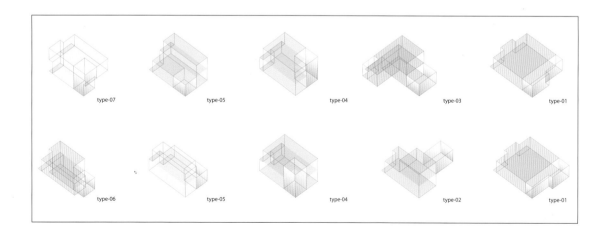

type-07    type-05    type-04    type-03    type-01

type-06    type-05    type-04    type-02    type-01

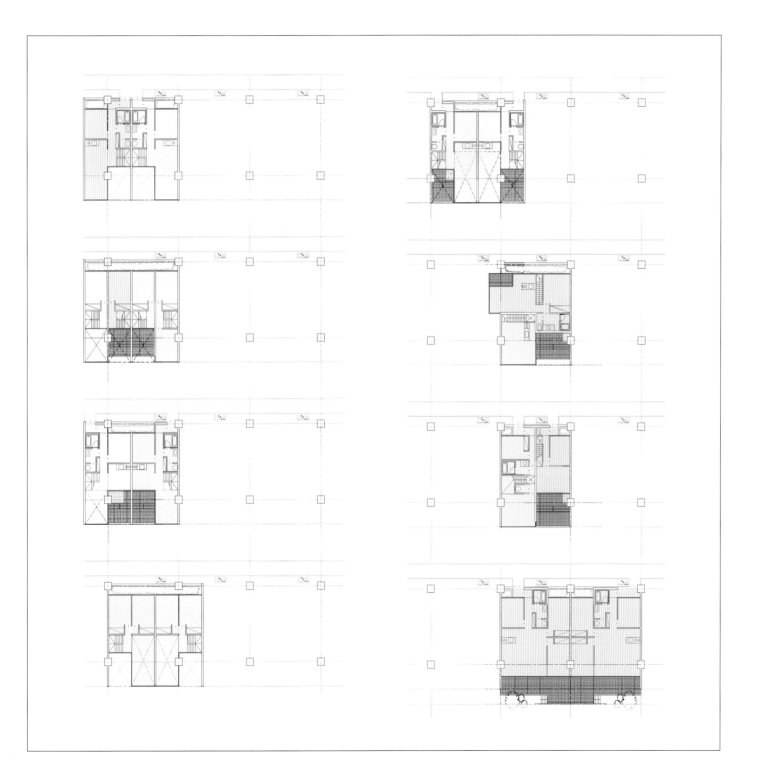

187

Site map of the residential complex; elevations of the three types of apartment.

Views of the models showing the three modes of combination.

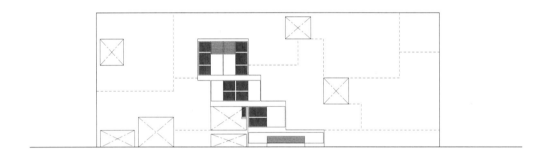

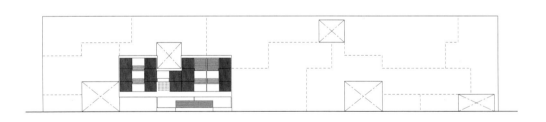

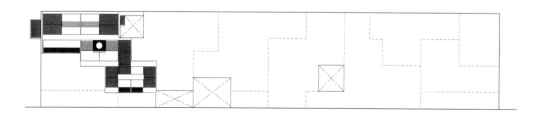

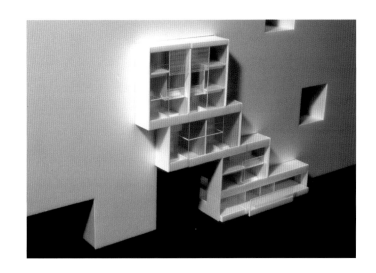

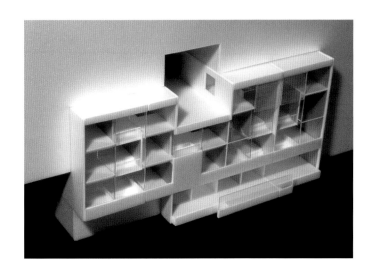

## LT Aoyama Building
Minato, Tokyo 2003

This is located in a highly fashionable district in the middle of Tokyo. The five-story building is occupied by a jewelry store on the first four floors and a salon for public relations and customer services on the top floor. Each floor in plan consists of just a single space and a stairway.

The tiny site is 6.30 meters wide, 4.60 meters deep, and less than 30 square meters in area. My two basic design ideas were to adopt a structural system without columns to make effective use of the limited area and to make the overall structure as lightweight as possible in order to simplify the foundation. A reinforced-concrete wall structure is used on the lower three floors. Panels fabricated from steel sheets in a factory were assembled on the site for the fourth and fifth floors. As a result, construction work was much like assembling a model of the building.

Grey pane glass, transparent glass and stainless mesh are layered on the façade of this urban building. The surface has the smoothness of glass but it also has the semblance of depth. Lighting installed between the overlapping materials gives the building a completely different look at night. This is an extremely small building, but I wanted it to be a delightful, jewel-like addition to the Tokyo townscape.

View of the model.

Digital model of the façades with the interior illuminated.

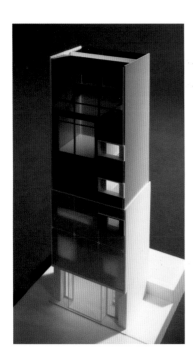

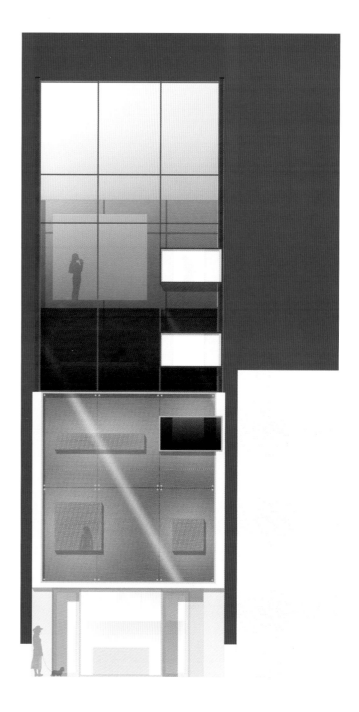

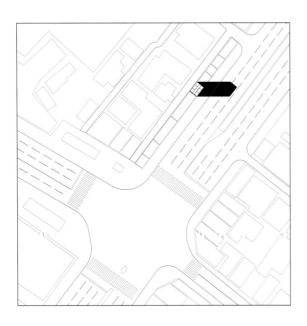

Site map; plans of the fourth
and ground floors; longitudinal
and cross sections.

Digital models of the interiors.

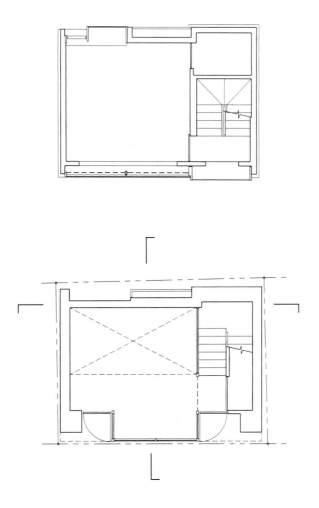

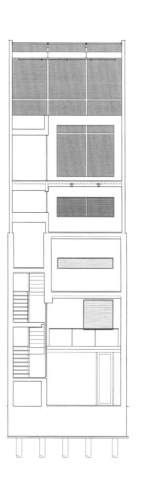

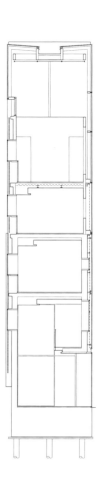

**installations and designs**

# Via Bus Stop Chain of Garment Stores
Shinjuku, Tokyo 1997 / Otaru, Hokkaido 1998–99 / Hakata, Fukuoka 1998–99

The theme underlying this series of shop designs was to employ "white" materials in producing a quiet, empty space suitable for the display of clothing. All three shops employ the same, minimal palette of materials—glass, aluminum, white marble, and white painted walls—to create a colorless, inorganic space. Yet I sought to give each shop an individual character in the way it related to the external space.

## Shinjuku, Tokyo
Shinjuku is a district of Tokyo symbolic of this city's vital, chaotic energy. Here I created a white space using a bare minimum of materials: white marble floors and walls of frosted glass with mirror backing. I wanted to produce a lucid space, aloof to the noise and confusion of the city.

## Otaru, Hokkaido
Here I introduced a device for indirectly summoning into the interior of the shop views of a harbor visible through apertures facing outwards. In an internal space created by using a bare minimum of materials, I placed screens composed of three layers: striped pattern glass, movable aluminum blinds with punching, and a roll screen of plain cloth. By manipulating the blinds and roll screens, the shop's apertures can be adjusted to various degrees of transparency or opacity to exterior light and views, so providing subtle control over the relationship of interior to exterior.

## Hakata, Fukuoka
In an interior composed as a white space, I introduced "talkative" materials, such as galvanized steel sheets and blue-tinted steel sheets with a hairline pattern, so creating a collection of contrasting spaces within a single shop. Each spatial unit, while independent, interconnects with the next. The shop interior is thus an assembly of spaces providing a sequential spatial experience

Interiors of Via Bus Stop men's garment store in Tokyo.

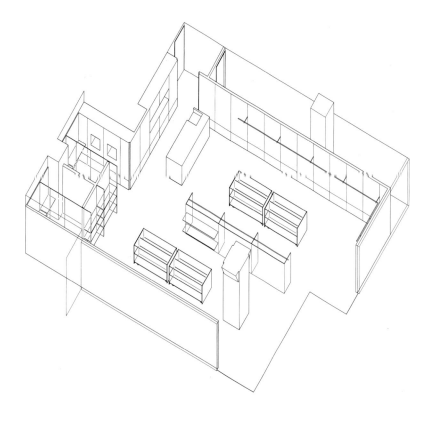

Axonometric projection and plan
of the interior.

View of the interior.

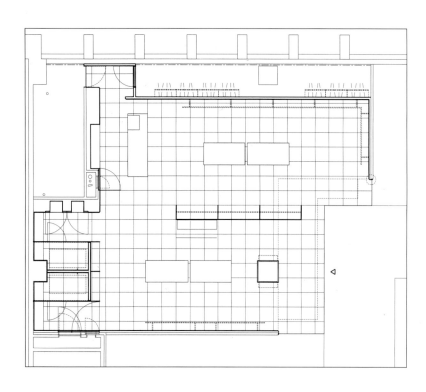

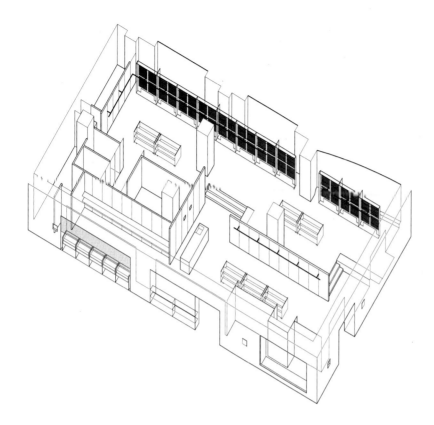

Axonometric projection and plan
of the Via Bus Stop store
at Hokkaido.

View of the interior.

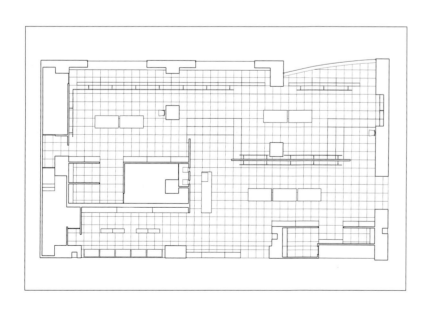

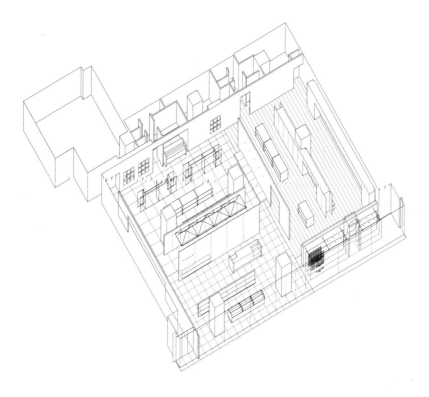

Axonometric projection and plan of the Via Bus Stop store at Fukuoka.

Views of the interior.

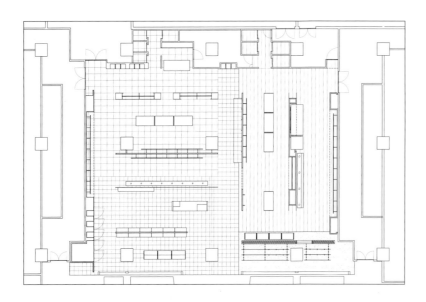

# Interior of the iCB Boutique
Paris 1998–99

This is a boutique on the ground floor of a nineteenth-century building in the Marolo area of Paris. The important point was to respect the character of the city: the landscape, the history, the irregular floor plan, and the façade, which is subject to conservation regulations. So I started the design by respecting the historical qualities of the building. While leaving the basic floor plan and façade, the existing balustrade and the cornices of the ceiling basically untouched, I introduced a thick plate of galvanized steel, a timber wall, frosted glass, black lacquer and aluminum furniture. With the minimal number of elements inserted, a space comes to life. I thought that through the minimum and the silent forms of materiality, it would be possible to confront the decorative culture of the city of Paris. Though it might sound like an exaggeration, this work is in a sense my attempt to show to how an Oriental architect can create possibilities in a European context.

Plan of the store.

Views of interiors.

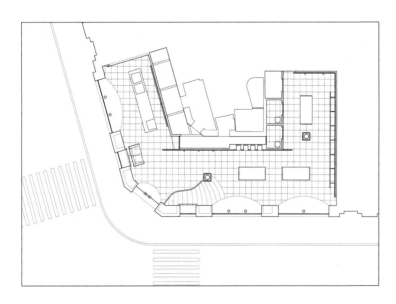

## Interior of Room 435
Atami, Shizuoka 2002

This is not a house: That was all I was thinking when I began designing this project. This space is, on the one hand, a place for spending time away from work, and on the other, the very opposite, namely a place to which work is brought. This is a place for spending both "idle time" and "work time"; the only thing forbidden in this place is immersion in the flow of everyday time, that is, "dwelling."

This space is therefore probably closest to a room in a hotel. A person can rest or work in a hotel room. A hotel room can be used in all sorts of ways. However, it can never be an "everyday space."

This project involved the remodeling of a condominium built over thirty years ago. The 43.5-square-meter unit was stripped of all its interior finishes. Then a shower/washbasin/toilet (there is no bath), a bed resembling a berth on a train, and a kitchen were arranged on one side. These functional spaces were made as small as possible in size, but their dimensions and tactile qualities were carefully considered. The remaining half of the unit is a space 2.9 meters wide and 10.5 meters deep: a deep, functionless space that is meant to be out of the ordinary in character. Beyond the window lies the Pacific Ocean.

By arranging functional spaces of minimal size that are almost smaller than humanly-scaled on the left side, I emphasized the deep space on the right side and the limitless ocean beyond. A single wall lined with dark brown wood panels of different lengths separates the two spaces. Looking back, I see that erecting the wall in a space of limitless extension was the one thing I wanted to do in this project.

Plan of the room.

View of the interior.

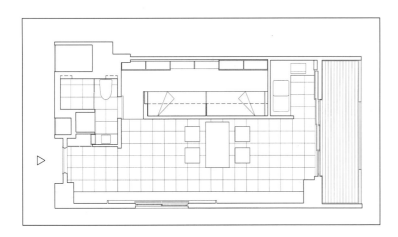

## Interiors of the Ono Store/Kyoto
Nakagyo, Kyoto 2003

Kyoto Ono is a "store" dealing in religious vestments and Buddhist altar articles for the Soto sect of Zen Buddhism. Business is not conducted here as in ordinary stores. First, the customers are mainly priests of the Soto sect. This is a place where talks are held with such persons, and the fact that vestments and articles are sold is secondary to those talks. Thus this was required to be, first of all, a space for conversations. The client wanted a space that was as unobtrusive as possible, a store that would not recognized as such by passersby, even though it stands on a major street in the middle of the city.

Designing this building was more like designing just the living room of a house or a hermitage in the middle of the city than designing a store. The place is indeed unlike other stores.

The space is defined by a number of surfaces. There are the horizontal surfaces of the floating *toko* alcove and tables. For these I used slightly unusual finishes: Japanese chestnut and zelkova with an adz finish. These are parts with which people come into direct contact, and I was especially careful in selecting the materials. There are three vertical surfaces. The first is a floating screen of steel plate situated on the inside of a pane of glass that is partly transparent and partly frosted. This screen, which shuts out views from the street and introduces only light, is made of six-millimeter thick steel plate with a "black rust" finish. The second is a brick wall in the middle of the space, and the third is an L-shaped surface of fabric.

The space is created only out of the three vertical surfaces—the solid and tensile surface of steel plate,

the hard and heavy wall of brick and the soft surface of fabric—and the two horizontal surfaces with quite different material qualities. My intention was to limit the elements to horizontal and vertical surfaces and to display a wealth of different material qualities in the space composed of those minimal elements.

Creating a retreat in the middle of the city means producing a space that is psychologically isolated in a place separated from the hustle and bustle of the city by only a single pane of glass or tens of centimeters in actual distance.

However, I am not at all certain that this constitutes the right solution for the store, which is named "Dogen" after the founder of the Soto sect. Given the exalted associations of this establishment, it seems arrogant of me even to suggest the possibility of a solution.

Axonometric projection of the shop.

View of the interiors.

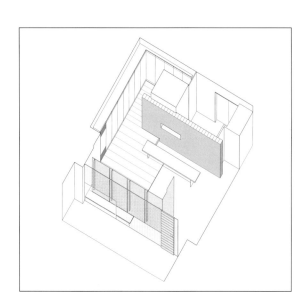

# Aqua Cube Furniture
Cassina, 2002–04

Aqua Cube is a line of furniture in acrylic. Acrylic is generally thought of, first of all, as a more transparent material than glass. It is also a material that is easily bent and bonded. This project had its origin in a desire on my part to demonstrate the attractions of acrylic as a material.

This furniture is made out of acrylic that has been made as thick as possible until it is almost massive; it has then been painted on its upper surface. The material as a whole is thus rendered opaque, but this has the effect of making the almost abstract colored surface underneath the thick acrylic quite conspicuous. That is, one sees this not as paint applied to acrylic, but as a thick, transparent finish applied on a colored surface. The presence of a flat, opaque plane of color emphasizes by contrast the transparency of the acrylic.

The form is basically a simple cuboid. I wanted the observer to consider only the materiality of acrylic. The legs were made as slender as possible; the acrylic thus seems to float in midair. The result is a cuboid as transparent as water, floating in midair, which is how it got its name Aqua Cube.

Through this project I learned acrylic has the luster and depth of Japanese lacquer. It came as a pleasant surprise to learn that this material was even more attractive and had even greater magical powers than I had imagined.

Views of the components made of acrylic.

on pages 212–13:
Digital models of the acrylic components.

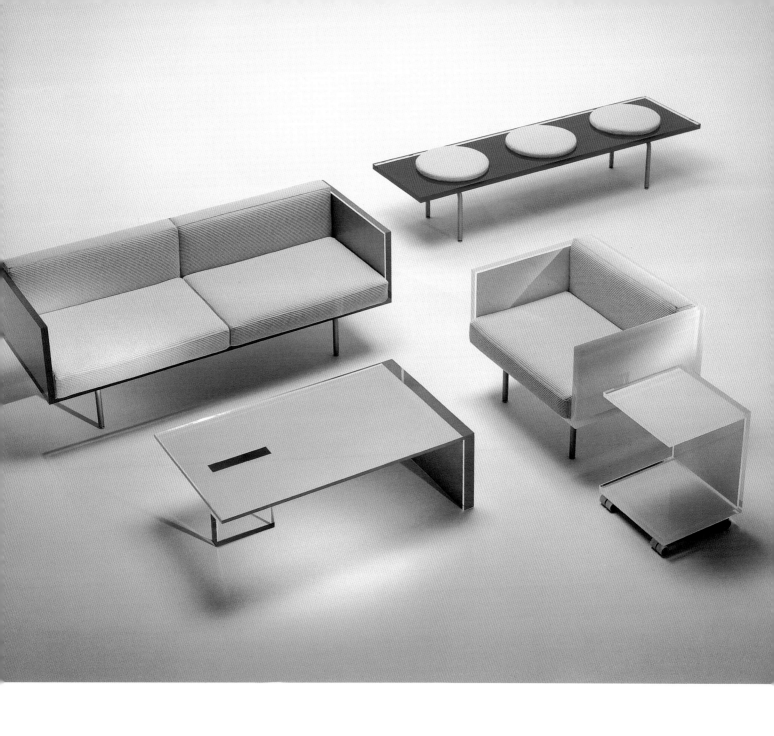

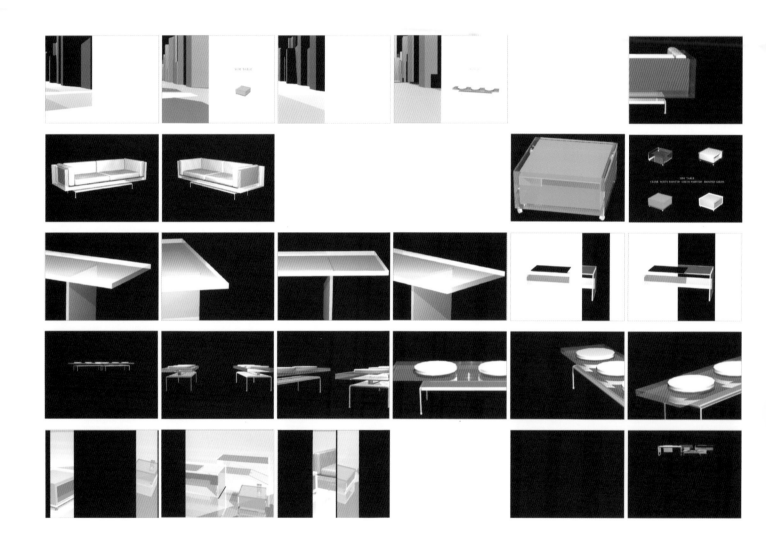

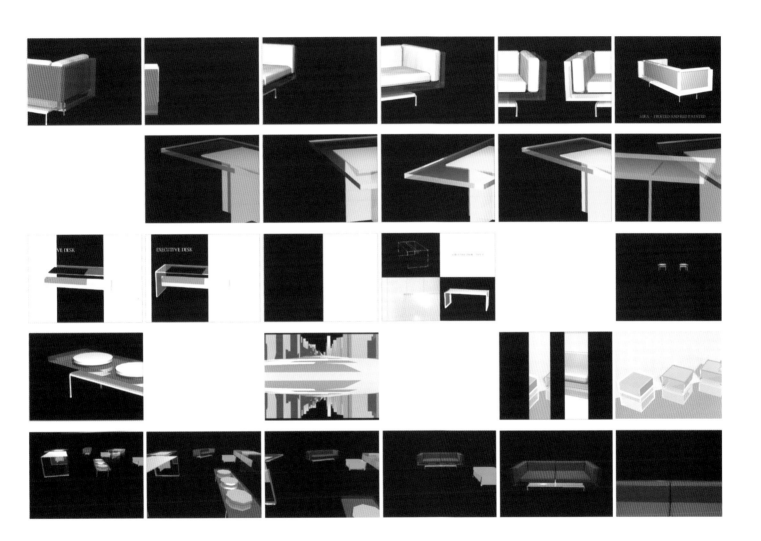

appendices

**chronology of works**

**"Wine Grocery" Liquor Store**
Shimogyo, Kyoto
project and completion: 1982

**Core 25 Club with Swimming Pool**
Kusatsu, Shiga
project: 1983–84
completion: 1984

**Kyoto College of Art, Takahara Campus**
Sakyo, Kyoto
project and completion: 1982

**Boutique Collection's**
Sumiyoshi, Osaka
project and completion: 1984

**M House**
Sakyo, Kyoto
project: 1983
completion: 1984

**Yamanouchi Liquor Store**
Minami, Kyoto
project and completion: 1984

**Dimaggio Boutique**
Sumiyoshi, Osaka
project and completion: 1984

**"Cloth and Yarn" Installation
at the World Ancient Castle Festival**
Hikone, Shiga
project: 1986–87
completion: 1987

**Interiors of the Nagano Natural History Museum**
Nagano
project: 1984–85
completion: 1985

**Kim House**
Ikuno, Osaka
project: 1986
completion: 1986–87

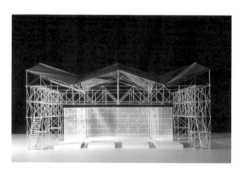

**Area for Events at the World Historic Cities Exposition**
Fushimi, Kyoto
project and completion: 1987

**Rakuhoku House**
Sakyo, Kyoto
project: 1987–88
completion: 1988–89

**Tsuzuki Apartment**
Chiyoda, Tokyo
project: 1988–89
completion: 1989

**Interiors of the Parade Bar**
Higashiyama, Kyoto
project and completion: 1989

**Auto Lab Car Showroom**
Ukyo, Kyoto
project and completion: 1989

**TS Chair**
project and completion: 1989

**Kyoto-Kagaku Research Institute**
Kizu, Kyoto
project: 1987–89
completion: 1989–90

**Kamigyo House**
Kyoto
project: 1988–90
completion: 1990

**Project for a Holiday House in Tateshina**
Nagano
project: 1991–92

**Yunoka Footbridge**
Ashikita, Kumamoto
project: 1989–90
completion: 1990–91

**"Ecclo" Watch**
project and completion: 1993

**House in Nipponbashi**
Naniwa, Osaka
project: 1990–91
completion: 1991–92

**Nakagyo House**
Kyoto
project: 1992–93
completion: 1993

**Sonobe SD Office Building**
Sonobe, Kyoto
project: 1991–92
completion: 1993

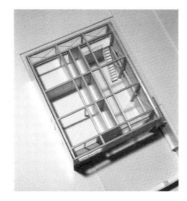

**Project for Y House**
Shiga
project: 1994

**House in Shimogamo**
Sakyo, Kyoto
project: 1992–94
completion: 1994

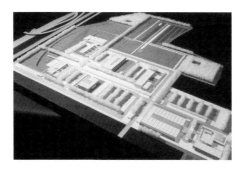

**Max Mara Headquarters Competition Project**
Reggio Emilia
project: 1994–95

**Sohka Restaurant**
Abeno, Osaka
project: 1993–94
completion: 1994

**Murasakino Wakuden Restaurant**
Kita, Kyoto
project: 1994
completion: 1995

**House in Takarazuka**
Hyogo
project: 1994–95
completion: 1995

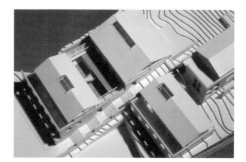

**Project for the N Wellness Center**
Hakone, Kanagawa
project: 1996–97

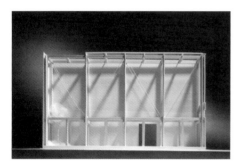

**Project for Store I**
Nakagyo, Kyoto
project: 1996–97

**Yamaguchi Memorial Hall**
Ube, Yamaguchi
project: 1994–96
completion: 1996–97

**Competition Project for the National Library Kansai Division**
Seika, Kyoto
project: 1996

**House in Higashi-Osaka**
Osaka
project: 1995–96
completion: 1996–97

**House in Higashinada**
Kobe
project: 1995–96
completion: 1996–97

**Interiors of the Via Bus Press Office**
Shibuya, Tokyo
project and completion: 1997

**Interiors of the Via Bus Stop Men's
Store in Shinjuku**
Tokyo
project and completion: 1997

**Project for the Music and Art Center in Jyvaskyla**
Finland
project: 1997

**Interiors of the Via Bus Stop Store in Namba**
Chuuou, Osaka
project: 1997–98
completion: 1998

**Interiors of the Via Bus Stop Accessories Store
in Shibuya-parco**
Tokyo
project: 1997–98
completion: 1998–99

**House in Kurakuen I**
Nishinomiya, Hyogo
project: 1996–97
completion: 1997–98

**Interiors of the Via Bus Stop Jeans Store
in Miyashitakoen–mae**
Shibuya, Tokyo
project: 1998
completion: 1998

**Project for the Araki gumi I + II Headquarters**
Okayama
project: 1996–98

**Interiors of the Via Bus Stop Store in Niigata**
Niigata
project and completion: 1998

**Interiors of the Via Bus Stop Store
in Kobe**
Hyogo
project: 1997–98
completion: 1998

**Interiors of the Via Bus Stop Store in Fukuoka**
Fukuoka
project: 1997–98
completion: 1998

**Interior of the iCB Boutique**
Paris
project: 1998
completion: 1998–99

**House in Suzaku**
Nara
project: 1996–97
completion: 1997–98

**Interiors of the Via Bus Stop Store in Hakata**
Fukuoka
project: 1998
completion: 1998–99

**Interiors of the Via Bus Stop Store in Shinjuku**
Tokyo
project and completion: 1997

**Interiors of the Via Bus Stop Assessories Store in Kobe**
Hyogo
project and completion: 1999

**Project for the Roswell Hotel**
Roswell, New Mexico
project: 1999

**Interiors of the Via Bus Stop Store in Nagoya**
Aichi
project: 1998
completion: 1999

**Interiors of the Via Bus Stop Store in Otaru**
Hokkaido
project: 1998
completion: 1999

**Project for the Aomori Museum**
Aomori
project: 1999–2000

**Interiors of the Via Bus Stop Jeans Store in Odaiba**
Kouto, Tokyo
project: 1998–99
completion: 1999

**Kazurasei Antique Gallery**
Nagayo, Kyoto
project: 1998–99
completion: 1999–2000

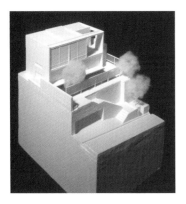

**Project for House in Karakuen III**
Nishinomiya, Hyogo
project: 2000

**Project for the 20 x 22 Meter House**
Kyoto
project: 1999–2000

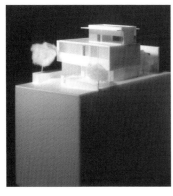

**Project for House in Karakuen IV**
Nishinomiya, Hyogo
project: 2000

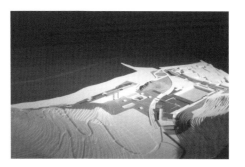

**Urban Project for the Teresitas Beachfront**
Santa Cruz de Tenerife, Canary Islands
project: 2000

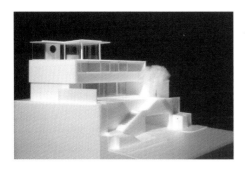

**Project for House in Karakuen V**
Nishinomiya, Hyogo
project: 2000

**House in Bunkyo**
Tokyo
project: 1999
completion: 2000

227

**House in Karakuen II**
Nishinomiya, Hyogo
project: 1996–97
completion: 2000–01

**House in Fukaya**
Saitama
project: 1999–2000
completion: 2000–01

**Stadium 1100 Pachinko Arcade**
Nagoya, Aichi
project: 2000–01
completion: 2001

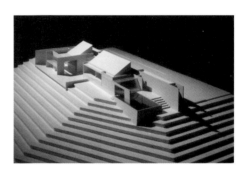

**House in the Rokko Mountains**
Hyogo
project: 2000–01

**Project for the Memorial Garden in Kyoto**
Kyoto
project: 2001

**Project for a House in Shinsaibashi**
Chuo, Osaka
project: 2001

**Stadium 600 Pachinko Arcade**
Nagoya, Aichi
project: 2000–01
completion: 2001

**Heiwabashi Bridge**
Hiroshima
project: 1995–2000
completion: 1999–2002

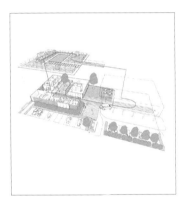

**Project for S Community Center**
Miyagi
project: 2001–02

**Project for Commercial Building
in Minami-Senba**
Tyuo, Osaka
project: 2002

**House in Sakai**
Osaka
project: 2001
completion: 2002

**Project for Housing in Sumoto**
Hyogo
project: 2002

**229**

**Competition Project for the Eda Housing Complex**
Yokohama, Kanagawa
project: 2002

**Interior of Room 435**
Atami, Shizuoka
project and completion: 2002

**House in Wakayama**
Wakayama
project: 2001
completion: 2001–02

**House in Higashi-Otsu**
Shiga
project: 2001–02
completion: 2002–03

**Hu-tong House**
Western Japan
project: 2001
completion: 2002

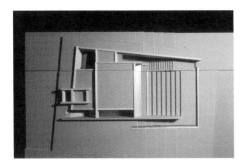

**Residence Annex for House K**
Aichi
project: 2002–03

**Interiors of the Ono Store/Kyoto**
Nakagyo, Kyoto
project and completion: 2003

**Competition Project for the Nam June Paik Museum**
Kyonggi, South Korea
project: 2003

**Project for Development of North Osaka**
Kita, Osaka
project: 2002–03

**Meridian Line Akashi Ferry Terminal**
Akashi, Hyogo
project: 2002–03
completion: 2003

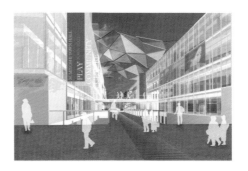

**Project for Sumiyoshi Community Hall**
Osaka
project: 2003

**Competition Project for the Kumano Forest Information Center**
Owase, Mie
project: 2003

**Paju SW Offices**
Seoul, South Korea
project: 2001–02
completion: 2002–04

**Standard House 2004**
Sakyo, Kyoto
project: 2003
completion: 2003–04

**Sumida Dental Clinic**
Amagasaki, Hyogo
project: 2002–03
completion: 2003–04

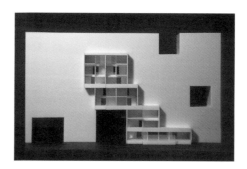

**Gifu Kitakata Housing**
Gifu
project: 2002
completion: in progress

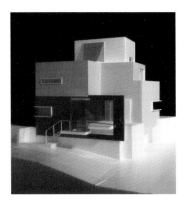

**House in Yoyogi-Uehara**
Tokyo
project: 2003
completion: in progress

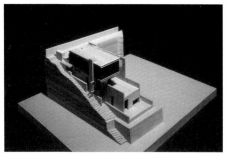

**House in Futako-Tamagawa**
Tokyo
project: 2003
completion: in progress

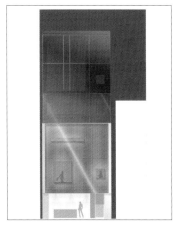

**LT Aoyama Building**
Minato, Tokyo
project: 2003
completion: in progress

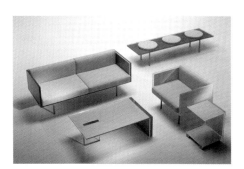

**Aqua Cube Furniture**
project and completion: 2002–04

# biography

**1950**
Born in Yokohama
**1973**
Graduated from Department
of Electronics, Kyoto University
**1975**
Graduated from Department
of Architecture, Kyoto University
**1978**
Completed post-graduate course
of Architecture, Kyoto University
**1981–93**
Principal, Waro Kishi, Architect &
Associates, Kyoto
**1981–93**
Taught Architectural Design at Kyoto
College of Art
**1993–**
Founded Waro Kishi
+ K. ASSOCIATES/Architects, Kyoto
**1993–2000**
Associate Professor, Kyoto Institute
of Technology
**2000–**
Professor, Kyoto Institute
of Technology

## Academic Experience
**1996–98**
Lecturer, Kyoto University, Kyoto
**2003**
Visiting Professor, University
of California, Berkeley
**2004**
Lecturer, Kyushu University, Fukuoka

Visiting Professor, Massachusetts
Institute of Technology, Cambridge

## Awards
**1983**
"Commercial Space Design Award
in Excellence," Japanese Society of
Commercial Space Designers, Tokyo
**1987**
"SD Review Award," Kajima Institute
Publishing Co., Ltd., Tokyo
**1991**
"Award for Townscape of Kumamoto
Prefecture," Kumamoto Prefectural
Government
**1993**
"JIA (Japan Institute of Architects)
Award for the Best Young Architect
of the Year," Japan Institute of
Architects, Tokyo
**1994**
"Hope Award for Excellent House
in Kyoto," Kyoto Municipal Government
**1995**
"Annual Architectural Design
Commendation of the Architectural
Institute of Japan," Architectural
Institute of Japan, Tokyo

"Kenneth F. Brown Asia Pacific
Culture and Architecture Merit Award,"
University of Hawaii, Honolulu
**1996**
"Annual Architectural Design
Commendation of the Architectural
Institute of Japan," Architectural
Institute of Japan, Tokyo

"The Prize of Architectural Institute
of Japan for Design," Architectural
Institute of Japan, Tokyo
**2002**
"Award for townscape of Aichi
Prefecture," Aichi Prefectural Government
**2004**
"Commercial Space Design Award
Nominate," Japanese Society of
Commercial Space Designers, Tokyo

## Exhibitions
**1986**
"Design New Wave '86," Japan Design
Committee, Tokyo
**1987**
"Japan Creative," Seibu Department
Store, Tokyo

"SD Review," Kajima Institute
Publishing Co., Ltd.,
Tokyo/Osaka/Kanazawa
**1989**
"Kagu Designers Week in Makuhari,"
The Conference for Japanese Culture
and Design, Chiba
**1990**
"Last Decade 1990," Japan Design
Committee, Tokyo

"Townhouse in Kyoto," Committee
for Exhibition on Townhouse in Kyoto,
Kyoto

"City of Yujo," Committee for City and
Architecture with Yujo, Tokyo/Osaka
**1992**
"Waro Kishi: Architectural Works
1987–1991," Gallery Kimi, Kyoto

"Waro Kishi: Architectural Works
1987–1991," Gallery Daishinsha,
Osaka
**1993**
"Tradition and Today," Japan Institute
of Architects, Kobe/Kyoto/Osaka

"Trans/Trance Chaos Tokyo,"
Architectural Design Conference
in Japan, Tokyo
**1994**
"Architects and Models," Japan
Institute of Architects, Tokyo

"Exhibition of JIA Award for the Best
Young Architect of the Year '94," Japan
Institute of Architects, Tokyo

"GA Japan League '94," GA Gallery,
Tokyo
**1995**
"Model for House," JIA Architectural
Seminar, Tokyo

"Emerging Trends in Contemporary
Japanese Architecture," Malaysian
Institute of Architects, Kuala Lumpur,
Malaysia

**1996**

"Emerging Trends in Contemporary Japanese Architecture," Institute of Siamese Architects, Bangkok, Thailand

"Emerging Trends in Contemporary Japanese Architecture," Mongolia Institute of Architects, Ulan Bator, Mongolia

"Venice Biennale: Sensing the Future," Venice

**1997**

"GA Houses Project 1997," GA Gallery, Tokyo

**1998**

"GA Houses Project 1998," GA Gallery, Tokyo

**1999**

"GA Houses Project 1999," GA Gallery, Tokyo

**2000**

"GA Houses Project 2000," GA Gallery, Tokyo

"East Wind 2000," Asia Design Forum, Tokyo

"GA Japan 2000," GA Gallery, Tokyo

"Projected Realities," Gallery MA, Tokyo

"Pacific Rim Architects," Pacific Rim Committee (Moderator: Waro Kishi), Tokyo

**2001**

"GA Houses Project 2001," GA Gallery, Tokyo

"New Trends of Architecture in Europe and Japan 2001," EU/JAPAN Committee for New Trends of Architecture in Europe and Japan, Tokyo, Japan/Porto, Portugal/Rotterdam, Netherlands

"Freehand Drawing of Architects," GA Gallery, Tokyo

"GA Japan 2001," GA Gallery, Tokyo

"Paju Book City," Paju Book City, Korea

**2002**

"GA Houses Project 2002," GA Gallery, Tokyo

"VIII Biennale," (representative for Japanese Pavilion), Venice

"TPO Recommendation 2002," TPO, Tokyo

"Architecture of Tomorrow," MA Gallery, Tokyo

**2003**

"GA Houses Project 2003," GA Gallery, Tokyo

"Architecture of Tomorrow," MA Gallery, Miyagi/Aichi/Ishikawa/ Hiroshima

**2004**

"Art Box Architectural Exhibition," Art Box Gallery, Tokyo

"Architecture of Tomorrow," MA Gallery, Kyoto/Fukuoka/ Yamagata

"GA Houses Project 2004," GA Gallery, Tokyo

"Contemporary Architects," The House Co. Ltd., Tokyo

**Conferences**

**1988**

*Conversation with Clients*, AXIS Inc., Tokyo

**1990**

*Townhouse in Kyoto*, Kyoto Culture Foundation, Kyoto Shimbun News, Kyoto

**1991**

*Recent Works*, Taisei Corporation, Nagoya

*Architecture and the City/City and Architecture*, Kyoto Municipal Office, Kyoto

*Architectural Forum in Tohoku/Poetics and Space*, Tohoku Institute of Technology, Sendai

**1992**

*Several Phases of Abstraction*, Kyoto Institute of Technology, Kyoto

**1993**

*On Modernism*, Osaka Society of Architects and Building Engineers, Osaka

*Open Symposium for the Urban Space*, Kansai Architects Conference, Osaka

*The Relationship between City and Architecture*, Japan Urban Design Institute, Osaka

*Die Hard Modernism*, Nagoya University, Nagoya

**1994**

*Recent Works*, Kinki University, Hiroshima

*Die Hard Modernism*, Japan Institute of Architects, Tokyo/Sendai

*Townhouse in Kyoto*, Kyoto Shimbun News, Kyoto

*Die Hard Modernism*, Kajima Corporation, Tokyo

**1995**

*On Recent Works*, Malaysian Institute of Architects, Kuala Lumpur, Malesia

*Recent Works*, Japan Institute of Architects, Osaka

*Die Hard Modernism*, Tsukuba University, Tsukuba

**1996**

*On Recent Works*, Institute of Siamese Architects, Bangkok, Thailand

*On Recent Works*, Canary Institute of Architects, Canary Islands, Spain

*Recent works*, Architectural Institute of Japan, Hakata

*Architecture and City*, Yamaguchi University, Yamaguchi

**1997**

*Recent Works*, Kyoto Institute of Technology, Kyoto

**1998**

*On Recent Works*, Japan Institute of Architects, Mie Prefectural Museum, Mie

*On Modernism in Architecture*, Yoshioka Foundation, Okinawa

**2000**

*On Recent Works*, Southern California Institute of Architecture, Los Angeles

*On Recent Works – Reading Urban Context*, Chinese University of Hong Kong, Hong Kong, China

*On Recent Works*, Seoul National University, Seoul, South Korea

*Postwar Architecture of Japan*, Japan Institute of Architects, Sendai

*On Recent Works*, Japan Institute of Architects, Hokkaido

*My Design Method*, Japan Institute of Architects, Yokohama

**2001**

*Conversation with the Authors*, Living Design Center, Tokyo

*On Recent Works*, Kobe Design University, Kobe

*Kyoto, my private landscape*, Japan Landscape Forum, Osaka

*On Recent Works*, Kyoto Art University, Kyoto

**2002**

*On Recent Works*, Michoacan University, Morelia, Mexico

*On Recent Works*, Peking University, Beijing, China

*On Recent Works*, Columbia University, New York

*On Recent Works*, XIII Chilean Biennale of Architecture, Santiago, Chile

*On Recent Works*, Japan Embassy in Chili, 21st Century Committee of Japan and Chili, Valparaiso, Chile

*On Recent Works*, Bolivia Catholic University, Santa Cruz, Bolivia

*On Recent Works*, University of California, Berkeley

*The End of Architecture*, MA Gallery, Tokyo

*Exhibition in Venezia Biennale*, The Japan Design Society, Kyoto

**2003**

*On Recent Works*, Royal Institute of Australian Architects 2003 National Conference, Sydney, Australia

*On Recent Works*, The 8th International Congress of Architecture, ITESM, Monterey, Mexico

*On Recent Works*, Yamaguchi Society of Architects and Building Engineers, Yamaguchi

*On Recent Works*, Hyogo Society of Architects and Building Engineers, Himeji

*On Recent Works*, Uruguay University, Kyoto

*On Recent Works*, Japan Institute of Architects, Kyoto

*On Recent Works*, Chuo College of Technology, Tokyo

*On Recent Works*, College of Industrial Technology, Nihon University, Tokyo

**2004**

*On Recent Works*, Seoul National University, Seoul, South Korea

*On Recent Works*, University of Texas in Austin, Austin, Texas

*The Characteristics and Perception of Space in Japan*, Japan Society, New York

*On Recent Works*, Parsons School of Design, New York

*On Recent Works*, Stuttgart Polytechnic, Stuttgart, Germany

*On Recent Works*, Osaka Sangyo University, Osaka

*Symposium on Landscape in Kyoto*, Institute for Historical City of Kyoto, Kyoto

*On Recent Works*, Aichi Society of Architects and Building Engineers, Aichi

# bibliography

## Monographs

**1992**

*Critic*, vol. 1, Osaka

*Waro Kishi: Architectural Works 1987–1991*, Tokyo

**1995**

*Waro Kishi*, Barcelona

**1996**

"Waro Kishi 1987–1996," *El Croquis*, 77–II

**1997**

*Case Study Houses*, Tokyo

"Waro Kishi Conception/Praxis," *Kenchiku Bunka*, vol. 52, 609

**2000**

*Waro Kishi*, Stuttgart

*Waro Kishi Projected Realities*, Tokyo

*Waro Kishi Store Design 5 Bus Stops + 1*, Modena

**2001**

*Cool Construction*, London

"Waro Kishi: Recent Works," *2G*, 19

**2003**

*The END of Architecture*, Tokyo

*Journey Through Architecture*, Tokyo

**2004**

*Waro Kishi*, Seoul

## Writings by Waro Kishi

**1982**

"Liquor Shop Wine Grocery," *Shoten Kenchiku*, vol. 27, 14, pp. 172–74

**1983**

translation by R. Banham, *Design by Choice*, Tokyo

"Kyoto College of Art/Takahara Division," *Shinkenchiku*, vol. 58, 5, pp. 195–99

"Liquor Shop Wine Grocery," *Annual of Display & Commercial Space Designs in Japan 1983*, Tokyo, pp. 162–63

**1984**

"Years of Emerging White-Colored Houses," *Kyoku*, 2, pp. 106–28

**1985**

translation by F. Dal Co, "Carlo Scarpa," *a+u*, pp. 14–43

"Liquor shop Yamanouchi," *Shoten Kenchiku*, vol. 30, 5, pp. 216–18

"Nowhere City/Architecture of Fumihiko Maki," *Kyoto Architecture Forum Exhibition Catalogue*, p. 1

"Space and Image (I)," *Shoten Kenchiku*, vol. 30, 11, p. 81

"Space and Image (II)," *Shoten Kenchiku* vol. 30, 12, p. 77

"Swimming Club Core 25," *Shoten Kenchiku*, vol. 30, 7, pp. 137–40

"Two Recent Works: Boutique Dimaggio, Boutique Collection's," *Shoten Kenchiku*, vol. 30, 8, pp. 162–67

**1986**

"Interior Design of Nagano Natural History Museum," *Annual of Display & Commercial Space Designs in Japan 1987*, Tokyo, p. 92

"Space and Image (III)," *Shoten Kenchiku*, vol. 31, 1, p. 79

**1987**

"Event Zone for World Historic Cities Exposition," *SD*, 279, pp. 28–29

"Event Zone for World Historic Cities Exposition," *Taiyo Special/Rekishi toshi*, p. 107

"Installation Cloth and Yarn," *Shitsunai*, 390, pp. 60–61

"Installation Cloth and Yarn," *Taiyo Special/Rekishi toshi*, p. 106

"Kim House," *SD*, 277, pp. 88–89

"Kim House," *Shinkenchiku/Jutakutokushu*, 18, pp. 118–21

**1988**

"Event Zone for World Historic Cities Exposition," *icon*, vol. 11, pp. 38–39

"Event Zone for World Historic Cities Exposition," *SD*, 400, p. 108

"Kim House," *Kenchiku Bunka*, vol. 43, 499, p. 128

"Kim House," *Kenchiku Chishiki*, vol. 30, 360, pp. 90–99

"Two Houses: Kim House, House Rakuhoku," *Shinkenchiku/Jutakutokushu*, 32, pp. 60–61

**1989**

translation by H. Plummer, "Fallingwater/Frank Lloyd Wright," *a+u*, pp. 137–39

"Exhibition report: Architecture of Tadao Ando," *SD*, 302, p. 93

"House Rakuhoku," *icon*, vol. 17, pp. 32–36

"House in Rakuhoku," *Shinkenchiku/Jutakutokushu*, 37, pp. 136–40

**1990**

"Auto Lab," *Shinkenchiku*, vol. 65, 2, pp. 303–07

"Bar Parade," *icon*, vol. 21, pp. 81–84

"Bar Parade," *Shoten Kenchiku*, vol. 35, 2, pp. 222–24

"Exhibition report: 13 Follies and Kashiihama Project," *Shinkenchiku/Jutakutokushu*, 54, p. 17

"House in Rakuhoku," *Kenchiku Bunka*, vol. 45, 523, p. 94

"Kyoto Kagaku Research Institute," *Nikkei Architecture*, 384, pp. 180–81

"Kyoto Kagaku Research Institute," *Shinkenchiku*, vol. 65, 11, pp. 336–43

"TS Chair," *Kagu Designer's Week Makuhari*, vol. 2, p. 39

"Tsuzuki Flat," *Shinkenchiku/Jutakutokushu*, 47, pp. 62–64

**1991**

"Architecture and City," *Talk of Design*, 2, pp. 64–71

"House in Japan '91: Three Houses," *Kenchiku Bunka*, vol. 46, 535, pp. 123–29

"On the Edge of Modernism/ House in Kamigyo," *Shinkenchiku/Jutakutokushu*, 58, pp. 69–75

"Tsuzuki Flat," *Jiyujikan*, 17, pp. 16–17

"Tsuzuki Flat," *Shitsunai*, 433, pp. 8–10, 60–61

"Will towards Architecture/Five Recent Works," *SD*, 322, pp. 101–24

"Yunoka Bridge," *SD*, 316, pp. 86–87

"Yunoka Bridge," *Shinkenchiku*, vol. 66, 12, pp. 316–20

**1992**

"The Dream of the Rooftop Garden/House in Nipponbashi," *Shinkenchiku/Jutakutokushu*, 74, pp. 25–34

"Emerging Idioms: About Modernism in Architecture/Three Recent Works," *The Japan Architect*, 6, pp. 156–67

"House in Nipponbashi," *Kenchiku Bunka*, vol. 47, 548, pp. 153–64

"House in Nipponbashi," *Shitsunai*, 452, p. 159

"Illusion, named Modernism," *Shinkenchiku*, vol. 67, 12, pp. 155–58

"Kyoto Kagaku Research Institute," *Domus*, 737, pp. 14–15

"Liquor Shop Wine Grocery," *Display Designs in Japan 1980–1990*, Tokyo, vol. 2, p. 153

"Making Japanese Space/Six Recent Works," *PSD*, vol. 21, pp. 12–18

"On Eileen Gray Architecture," *Shinkenchiku/Jutakutokushu*, 75, pp. 76–77

"Space analyses of Maekawa's Kinokuniya Bookstore Building," *SD*, 331, pp. 20–25

"Two Houses: House in Kamigyo, House in Nipponbashi," *Shitsunai*, 447, pp. 18–19, 60, 64

"Yunoka Bridge," *Kumamoto Artporis '92 Collection*, Kumamoto, p. 38

Yunoka Bridge," *Kumamoto Artporis Guide Book*, Kumamoto, pp. 56–57

"Yunoka Bridge," *Nikkei Construction*, 58, pp. 118–23

"Yunoka Bridge," *Shitsunai*, 455, p. 19

"Yunoka Bridge," *Urban Design 12 Cities*, Tokyo, p. 187

**1993**

"Changing Phases of Modernism: Problematic of Houses/Five Houses," *Jutaku Kenchiku*, 221, pp. 40–73

"House in Nipponbashi," *Detail*, vol. 33, 01, pp. 29–31

"House in Nipponbashi," *GA Japan*, 02, pp. 172–75

"Kyoto Kagaku Research Institute," *Front*, vol. 5, 7, pp. 26–27

"Kyoto, my hometown," *All Kansai*, 221, p. 58

"Notes on Japanese City: From Central Court to Rooftop Garden/Three Houses," *Quaderns*, 202, pp. 56–77

"Sonobe SD Office," *Kenchiku Bunka*, vol. 48, 556, pp. 36–37

"Two Office: Kyoto Kagaku Research Institute, Sonobe SD Office," *The Japan Architect*, 11, pp. 178–87

"Yunoka Bridge," *Nikkei Architecture*, 471, p. 85

"Yunoka Bridge," *The Japan Architect*, 10, pp. 218–22

**1994**

"Architecture as Instrument," *GA Japan*, 7, pp. 67–68

"Bar Parade," *Shoten Kenchiku Extra Edition*, 4, p. 33

"City, named Landscape/House in Nakagyo," *Shinkenchiku/Jutakutokushu*, 93, pp. 17, 38–49

"Die Hard Modernism," *Kenchiku Bunka Kouenkaishu*, pp. 30–39

"Future of the Game," *The Japan Architect*, 14, pp. 138–39

"House in Nakagyo," *GA Houses*, 40, pp. 132–39

"House in Nakagyo," *Nikkei Architecture*, 502, p. 126

"House in Shimogamo," *GA Houses*, 44, pp. 110–21

"Kim House," *Architecture and Society*, vol. 75, 1, p. 51

"Landscape and Transparency/Sonobe SD Office," *Shinkenchiku*, vol. 69, 3, pp. 195–203

"Logical Spaces: Three Recent Works," *Casabella*, vol. 613, pp. 4–15

"Memorial Hall in Yamaguchi," *GA Japan*, 11, pp. 102–03

"Office space/Sonobe SD Office," *Kenchiku Bunka*, vol. 49, 569, pp. 105–13

"On Modernism," *JIA News*, 7, p. 10

"Rooftop Garden/House in Nakagyo," *Kenchiku Bunka*, vol. 49, 567, pp. 125–32

"Sonobe SD Office," *Nikkei Architecture*, 484, pp. 160–63

"Two Recent Works: Sonobe SD Office, House Nakagyo," *GA Japan*, 07, pp. 46–66

**1995**

"Five Glass Houses, On Steel-Frame Construction," *Shinkenchiku/Jutakutokushu*, 111, pp. 27–33

"Future of the Game/Two Recent Works: Sonobe SD Office, House in Shimogamo," *a+t*, 6, pp. 18–38

"House in Nipponbashi," *Sakuhin Senshu 1994–1995*, Tokyo, pp. 40–41

"House in Shimogamo," *Bauwelt*, 42/43, pp. 76–77

"House in Shimogamo," *Domus*, 772, pp. 24–29

"House in Takarazuka," *GA Houses*, 45, pp. 116–17

"In Hong Kong," *at*, 114, p. 3

"Kyoto–Kagaku Research Institute," in *Urban Design*, Hyogo Prefectural Government, p. 37

"Max Mara Headquarters," *The Japan Architect*, 19, pp. 216–23

"Modern Architecture/House in Shimogamo," *Shinkenchiku/Jutakutokushu*, 105, pp. 42–53

"On Architecture," *Archi-Forum in Osaka*, vol. 3, pp. 13–14

"On Frank Lloyd Wright," *at*, 104, p. 50

"Restaurant Sohka," *Domus*, 775, pp. 44–47

"Restaurant Sohka," *Shinkenchiku*, vol. 70, 3, pp. 224–28

"Sonobe SD Office," *Nikkei Architecture*, 514, p. 45

"Sonobe SD Office," *The Japan Architect*, 17, pp. 64–65

"Three Recent Works: Waro Kishi," *Modern*, Tokyo, pp. 122–29

"Tsuzuki Flat," *Confort*, 21, pp. 58–59

"Yunoka Bridge," *Keikan Zairyo*, 09, p. 27

"Yunoka Bridge," *SD*, 371, pp. 56–57

**1996**

"Changing Phases of Modernism: About Urban Houses/Five Recent Works," *Jutaku Kenchiku*, 259, pp. 118–65

"Discovery of Suburban/House in Takarazuka," *Shinkenchiku/Jutakutokushu*, 117, pp. 45–54

"History and contemporariness in Modern Era," *El Croquis*, pp. 6–17

"Homage to White-Coloured Houses: Architecture of Kameki Tuchiura," *SD*, 382, pp. 61–66

"House in Higashinada," *GA Houses*, 48, pp. 78–79

"House in Kurakuen I," *Shinkenchiku/Jutakutokushu*, 128, p. 39

"House in Nipponbashi," *Contemporary Housing Design*, 1, pp. 112–15

"House in Shimogamo," *Innovation in Steel*, p. 19

"House in Takarazuka," *GA Japan*, 19, pp. 32–39

"House in Takarazuka," *The Japan Architect*, 24, pp. 164–65

"I dream of Architecture," *Kenchiku Bunka*, vol. 51, 600, p. 1

"Kyoto-Kagaku Research Institute," *Laboratories & Research Facilities*, Tokyo, pp. 194–99

"New Generation of Architecture in West Japan: Four Recent Works," *Ideal Architecture*, 9605, pp. 140–51

"On Architecture in Detail," *The Japan Architect*, 23, pp. 4–6

*Recent Works: On Nature, City and Architecture/Four Houses*," *Shinkenchiku/Jutakutokushu*, 123, pp. 103–17

"Restaurant Murasakino Wakuden," *Commercial Facilities*, Tokyo, pp. 164–70

"Restaurant Murasakino Wakuden," *GA Japan*, 18, pp. 126–31

"Restaurant Murasakino Wakuden," *Shinkenchiku*, vol. 71, 1, pp. 176–87

"Restaurant Sohka," *Bauwelt*, 39, pp. 56–57

"Sonobe SD Office," *Kenchiku Magazine*, vol. 111, 1385, pp. 44–45

"Sonobe SD Office," *Office Buildings*, Tokyo, pp. 108–14

"Sonobe SD Office," *Sakuhin senshu 1996*, Architectural Institute of Japan, pp. 44–45

"Tsuzuki Flat," *Axis*, vol. 64, pp. 111–15

"Two Houses: House in Nipponbashi, House in Shimogamo," *Catalogue of Venezia Biennale, 6th International Architecture Exhibition*, Milan, pp. 200–01

"Two Restaurants: Restaurant Sohka, Restaurant Murasakino Wakuden," *Diseño Interior*, 54, pp. 94–101

"Yunoka Bridge," Joan Roig, *Nuevos Puentes–New Bridges*, Barcelona, pp. 126–33

**1997**

"City Disappears: Architecture Exists/Two Houses: House in Higashinada, House in Higashi-osaka," *Shinkenchiku/Jutakutokushu*, 135, pp. 20–43

"Conception/Praxis," *Kenchiku Bunka*, vol. 52, 609, p. 186

"The Detail of Terragni, or a form Analysis of Casa del Fascio," *INAX Corporation*, 15, pp. 154–63

"Four Houses: Kim House, House in Kamigyo, House in Nipponbashi, House in Shimogamo," *Lotus*, 92, pp. 31–33, 44–49

"House in Higashinada," *Town Houses*, Barcelona, pp. 152–61

"House in Higashi-osaka," *GA Japan*, 25, pp. 96–97

"House in Higashi-osaka," *International Architecture Yearbook*, 4, pp. 344–45

"House in Nipponbashi," *Contemporary Japanese Architecture 1985–1996*, exhibition catalogue, p. 8

"House in Nipponbashi," *SD*, 390, pp. 33–36

"House in Nipponbashi," *UME 4*, pp. 58–63

"House in Shimogamo," *Kenchiku Chishiki*, vol. 39, 1, pp. 56–57, 132–33

"House in Takarazuka," *Detail*, vol. 37, 02, pp. 169–72

"JIA Award for the Best Young Architect of the Year Comment," *JIA News*, 103, pp. 3–4

"Memorial Hall in Yamaguchi," *GA Japan*, 27, pp. 126–33

"Memorial Hall in Yamaguchi," *Shinkenchiku*, vol. 72, 7, pp. 132–45

"Restaurant Murasakino Wakuden," *Detail*, vol. 37, 08, pp. 1330–32

"Sonobe SD Office," *Data File of Architectural Design & Detail*, 62, pp. 159–64

"Three Houses: House in Shimogamo, Restaurant Sohka, House in Takarazuka," *Arquine*, 1, pp. 34–45

"Two Houses: House in Higashi-osaka, House in Higashinada," *GA Houses*, 53, pp. 106–21

**1998**

"House in Higashi-osaka," *Capital*, 7, pp. 102–03

"House in Higashi-osaka," *Moebel Interior Design*, 4668, pp. 16–20

"House in Higashi-osaka," Peter Zellner, *Pacific Edge*, London, pp. 16–21

"House in Kurakuen I," *GA Japan*, 33, pp. 138–45

"House in Kurakuen I," *Shinkenchiku/Jutakutokushu*, 147, pp. 56–66

"House in Suzaku," *GA Houses*, 58, pp. 98–109

"House in Suzaku," *GA Japan*, 31, pp. 86–87

"Judge's Pleasure," *Compe & Contest*, 59, p. 26

"Memorial Hall in Yamaguchi," *Casabella*, 657, pp. 16–21

"National Library Kansai Division," *Il Progetto*, 3, pp. 12–14

"National Library Kansai Division," *Kenchiku Chishiki*, vol. 40, 1, pp. 118–19

"On Lectures by Architects," *Kenchiku Magazine*, vol. 113, 1431, pp. 30–31

"Restaurant Murasakino Wakuden," Willian Lin, Tan Hock S.W. and Beng, *Contemporary Vernacular*, Singapore, pp. 128–33

"Steel-Frame Construction Today,"
*Jutaku Kenchiku Extra Edition*, 48,
pp. 4–7

"Toward a 20th-Century Vernacular,"
*The Japan Architect*, 29, pp. 8–10

**1999**

"Antique Gallery Kazurasei," *GA
Japan*, 40, pp. 108–11

"House in Higashinada,"
*L'architecture d'aujourd'hui*, 320,
pp. 112–13

"House in Higashi-osaka," Philip
Jodidio, *Building a New Millennium*,
Cologne, pp. 280–83

"House in Kurakuen II," *GA Houses*,
59, pp. 98–101

"House in Ohimogama,"
*Shinkenchiku*, vol. 74, 6, p. 229

"House in Suzaku," *The Japan
Architect*, 34, pp. 110–19

"Material and Color of the
Contemporary Architecture,"
*Toyo-Ink News*, 75, pp. 32–34

"Memorial Hall in Yamaguchi,"
*Detail*, 142, p. 126

"Memorial Hall in Yamaguchi,"
*Lotus*, 102, pp. 88–91

"On Architectural Works," *Kenchiku
Magazine*, vol. 114, 1442, p. 20

"On Conservatism in Architecture,"
*Shinkenchiku*, vol. 74, 5, pp. 66–71

"Restaurant Murasakino Wakuden,"
*Detail*, 140, p. 126

"Technology and Urban Space:
Architecture of Shoji Hayashi,"
*INAX Report*, 138, pp. 6–8

"To Design a House/House in
Suzaku," *Shinkenchiku/Jutakutokushu*,
153, pp. 26–38

"Two Restaurants: Restaurant Sohka,
Restaurant Murasakino Wakuden,"
*Bars & Restaurants*, Barcelona,
pp. 116–23

**2000**

"Answering the Question of
Modernism," David N. Buck,
*Responding to Chaos*, London,
pp. 86–97

"Antique Gallery Kazurasei," *GA
Japan*, 44, pp. 140–49

"Courtyard Roof Garden/House in
Bunkyo," *Shinkenchiku/Jutakutokushu*,
175, pp. 58–75

"House in Bunkyo," *GA Houses*, 65,
pp. 92–101

"House in Bunkyo," *Shitsunai*, 552,
pp. 34–35

"House in Shimogamo," Carles Broto,
*Domestic Interiors*, Barcelona,
pp. 214–21

"Place where Architecture Exists,"
*Shinkenchiku*, vol. 75, 6,
pp. 126–27

"Pleasure of Moving," *Shinkenchiku*,
vol. 75, 13, pp. 168–69

"Roswell Hotel," *Monument
Millennium Special Issue*, p. 27

"Travel in Spain," *INAX Report*,
145, p. 2

"Two Recent Works: Antique Gallery
Kazurasei, iCB Paris," Shinkenchiku,
vol. 72, 5, pp. 110–25

"Via Bus Stop Otaru," *Shoten
Kenchiku*, vol. 45, 2, pp. 130–33

**2001**

"About Architect," *Tokyo-jin*, 164,
p. 65

"Case Study House," *Casa Brutus*,
16, pp. 27–30

"Four Recent Works," Raymund Ryan,
*Cool Construction*, London-Tokyo,
pp. 47–71

"House by Kazuhiro Kojima," *GA
Houses*, 73, pp. 120–23

"House in Fukaya," *GA Japan*, 52,
pp. 56–63

"House in Fukaya,"
*Shinkenchiku/Jutakutokushu*, 185,
pp. 18–33

"House in Kurakuen II," *GA Houses*,
67, pp. 17–29

"House in Kurakuen II,"
*Shinkenchiku/Jutakutokushu*, 181,
pp. 76–85

"House in Nipponbashi," *The House
Book*, London, p. 230

"House in Suzaku," Philip Jodidio,
*Architecture Now!*, Köln, vol. 1,
pp. 320–25

"Intention in Architecture," *INAX
Report*, 149, pp. 4–7

"Pacific Rim Architects," *a+u*, 368,
p. 128

"Restaurant Sohka," *Contemporary
Commercial Space in Japan*, Beijing,
pp. 36–37

"Tradition and Contemporariness,"
*2G*, 19, pp. 138–42

"Two Houses: House in Suzaku,
House in Bunkyo," *Lotus*, 111,
pp. 36–47

**2002**

"Birth of Architecture," *Shinkenchiku*,
vol. 77, 9, pp. 47–49

"Drama-like Space/Stadium 600,"
*Shinkenchiku*, vol. 77, 1, pp. 164–71

"House in Fukaya,"
*Shinkenchiku/Jutakutokushu*, 194,
pp. 62–93

"House in Fukaya," *The Gold*, 233,
pp. 38–40

"House in Fukaya," *The Japan
Architect*, 44, pp. 22–23

"House in Higashinada," *Detail*, 152,
pp. 52–53

"House in Higashi-osaka," *PreFab*,
Barcelona, pp. 66–71

"House in Sakai," *GA Japan*, 56,
pp. 132–41

"House in Suzaku," Christian Schittich,
*Japan*, Basel, pp. 118–19

"House in Wakayama," *GA Houses*,
72, pp. 60–75

"Hu-tong House," *GA Houses*, 72,
pp. 76–91

"On courtyard/Three Houses by Waro
Kishi," *Shinkenchiku/Jutakutokushu*
199, pp. 53–81

"Stadium 600," *GA Japan*, 54,
pp. 62–71

"The Meridian Line Akashi Ferry
Terminal," *GA Japan*, 59,
pp. 156–159

"Two Houses: House in Kurakuen II,
House in Fukaya," *Domus*, 845,
pp. 72–81

"Two Houses: House in Kurakuen II,
House in Fukaya," Philip Jodidio,
*Architecture Now!*, Cologne, vol. 2,
pp. 296–307

"Two Houses: House in Kurakuen II,
House in Fukaya," *Interior World
Magazine*, 26, pp. 62–65

**2003**

"House in Fukaya," Janme Nasple,
*Kyoto Anohura, Minimalist Interiors*,
Barcelona, pp. 170–75

"House in Higashi-Otsu," *GA Houses*,
74, pp. 124–25

"House in Higashi-Otsu," *GA Houses*,
75, pp. 106–15

"House in Higashi-Otsu,"
*Shinkenchiku/Jutakutokushu* 208,
pp. 18–27

"Hu-tong House," *Arquitectura Viva*,
102, pp. 52–55

"Hu-tong House," *Domus*, 862,
pp. 90–99

"Interiors Design: Four Via Bus Stops,"
*Lotus*, 118, pp. 102–11

"Stadium 600," *Graphis*, 338,
pp. 78–82

"The Meridian Line Akashi Ferry
Terminal," *GA Japan*, 65,
pp. 60–65

"The Meridian Line Akashi Ferry
Terminal," *Shinkenchiku*, vol. 78, 11,
pp. 82–89

"Three Recent Works: Yunoka Bridge,
Stadium 600, House in Wakayama,"
*Architecture & Design*, 105,
pp. 132–39

"Waro Kishi Special: On Architecture
in Detail/Four Recent Works,"
*Archiworld*, 102, pp. 56–89

"Whiteness of Claesson Koivisto
Rune," *Nine Houses*, Kyoto,
pp. 10–11

"Will towards Architecture, Modernism
Architecture," *INAX Corporation*,
pp. 180–90

"Yunoka Bridge," *Kumamoto Artpolis*,
pp. 60–61

**2004**

"House in Fukaya," *Art Box in Japan*,
Tokyo, vol. 1, pp. 98–99

"House in Fukaya," *Detail*, 159,
pp. 18–19

"House in Higashi-Otsu," *The Japan
Architect*, 52, pp. 89–90

"House in Wakayama," Joseph Cali,
*The New Zen Garden*, Tokyo,
pp. 60–61

"House in Wakayama," Cynthia
Reschke, *Pacific House*, Barcelona,
pp. 100–07

"House-Standard 2004,"
*Shinkenchiku/Jutakutokushu*, 217,
pp. 28–37

"K Residence Annex," *GA Houses*,
80, pp. 74–75

"Paju SW office," *Shinkenchiku*,
vol. 79, 7, pp. 109–15

"Roswell Hotel," *Interiors*, 208,
p. 227

"Stadium 600," *Casa Brutus*, 48,
p. 176

"Sumida Dental Clinic," *GA Japan*,
68, pp. 102–07

"Sumida Dental Clinic," *Shinkenchiku*,
vol. 79, 5, pp. 141–46

"Three Houses: Hu-tong House,
House in Wakayama, House in Sakai,"
*Interior World Magazine*, 29,
pp. 43–63

"Three Recent Works: Antique Gallery
Kazurasei, House in Bunkyo, House
in Nakagyo," *Naujas Namas*, 21,
pp. 28–42

"Two Houses: House in Fukaya,
Hu-tong House," *The Phaidon Atlas
of Contemporary World Architecture*,
London, pp. 146, 179

"Two Recent Works: Via Bus Stop
Otaru, Restaurant Murasakino
Wakuden," *Shop & Retail*, 25,
pp. 56–57, 98–99

"Via Bus Stop Otaru," *Shoten
Kenchiku Extra Edition*, pp. 70–71

"Zen lounge Ono/Kyoto," *GA Japan*,
66, pp. 136–41

"Zen lounge Ono/Kyoto," *Shinkenchiku*,
vol. 79, 1, pp. 162–65

**Writings on Waro Kishi**

**1990**

H. Nakahara, "Urban House by Waro
Kishi," *Urban House on Will*, Tokyo,
pp. 434–43

"On Waro Kishi's Houses,"
*Jutakuryutsu Shimbun*, March 23

"Space to Feel Happiness," *The
Mainichi Newspapers*,

June 31

**1991**

M. Furuyama, "Far from Emotion,"
*SD*, 322, pp. 110–11

T. Sakaiya, Moriteru Hosokawa,
"Vitalization for Countrysides,"
*President*, vol. 29, 11, p. 201

N. Suzuki, "Vitalization for
Countrysides: Yunoka Bridge,"
*Brutus*, vol. 12, 23, p. 11

*On Contemporary Architecture*,
"Asahi Shimbun," January 19

"Sampling of Designs," *Last Decade*,
Tokyo, p. 102

**1992**

S. Hashizume, "On the Exhibition
of Waro Kishi,"
*Shinkenchiku/Jutakutokushu*, 75,
p. 10

T. Oshima, "On the Exhibition
of Waro Kishi," *Kenchiku Bunka*,
vol. 47, 548, p. 14

Y. Takehara, "On the Exhibition of Waro Kishi," *Shinkenchiku*, vol. 67, 6, p. 194

"Exhibition and Monograph," *Shitunai*, 448, p. 147

"In Keihanshin Area," *Shitunai*, 450, p. 49

"Landscape in Kyoto," *Nikkei Architecture*, vol. 425, p. 57

"Post-Modernism Architecture," *Brutus*, vol. 13, 15, p. 69

**1993**

R. Takase, "Yunoka Bridge: Relationship between Kumamoto Artpolis and the Citizens," *Architecture Magazine*, 77, p. 26

"Cinema and Architecture," *Architecture and Society*, vol. 74, 856, p. 82

"Hope Award for Excellent House in Kyoto: House in Nakagyo," *Competition of House in Kyoto*, Kyoto, pp. 12–13

"JIA Awards for the Best Young Architect of the Year," *Nikkei Architecture*, 468, p. 35

"On Recent Works," *Shitunai*, 462, p. 139

**1994**

D. Chipperfield, "Making Space," *Casabella*, 613, p. 5

M. Furuyama, "End of Postmodernism/New Conservatism," *Mainichi Shimbun*, February 3

"28 Contemporary Architects," *Modern Living*, 94, p. 194

"Designing of Townscape: House in Nakagyo," *Guidebook of Townhouse in Kyoto*, vol. 60342, p. 50

"JIA Awards for the Best Young Architect of the Year," *Nikkei Architecture*, 484, p. 193

**1995**

T. Azuma, "Space of Penthouse: House in Nipponbashi," *Ryusei*, 423, pp. 32–35

"Annual Architectural Design Commendation of the Architectural Institute of Japan," *Kenchiku Magazine*, vol. 110, 1376, p. 71

"37 Architects in Japan," *Kateigaho*, vol. 38, 6, p. 364

"Kitchens with Big Tables: House in Shimogamo," *Modern Living*, 101, pp. 86–87

"On Waro Kishi's Works, *581 Architects in the World*, Tokyo, p. 563

"Sense of the City and Townhouse in Kyoto: House in Nakagyo," *Gas News*, 208, pp. 17–18

**1996**

M. Ueda, in "Contemporary Housing Design," *Sumairon*, 37, pp. 57–58

"Annual Architectural Design Commendation of the Architectural Institute of Japan," *Kenchiku Magazine*, vol. 111, 1388, p. 95

"The Prize of The Architectural Institute of Japan for Design," *Kenchiku Magazine*, vol. 111, 1393, pp. 58–59

**1997**

N. Maki, "Waro Kishi: International Style," *Kenchikuchoryu 05*, Kyoto, pp. 142–45

H. Nishizawa, "On Structural Design of the Memorial Hall in Yamaguchi," *Kenchiku Magazine*, vol. 112, 1412, pp. 18–19

E. Yamamori, "House in Higashi-osaka," *Asahi Shimbun*, July 27

"Case Study House," *Shitunai*, 514, p. 142

"Questions on Architecture and Architectural Technology," *The Kenchiku Gijutsu*, 562, pp. 203–04

"Restaurant Wakuden," *Mrs.*, 505, pp. 94–95

**1998**

D.N. Buck, "Architecture and Design," *The Japan Times*, February 8

**1999**

T.H. Beng, "Rising Son," *Men's Folio*, 378, pp. 48–52

**2000**

T. Riley, "Det o- Privatahuset," *mama*, 27, p. 94

H. Watanabe, "An Architect disguised as a Modernist," *Waro Kishi, Buildings and Projects*, Stuttgart, pp. 6–15

**2001**

T. Heneghan, "Eloquent White," *2G*, 19, pp. 4–25

**2002**

N. Suzuki, "104 Architects in Japan," *Houses and Architects*, Tokyo, p. 223

N. Suzuki, "Five Contemporary Collective Housing," *Brutus*, vol. 23, 17, p. 97

"50 Contractors Recommended by Architects," *Shitunai*, 565, p. 79

"Stadium 600 as a Landmark," *Amusement Japan*, vol. 5, 40, pp. 98–99

**2003**

N. Hino, "A Portrait of Waro Kishi," *GA Houses*, vol. 73, pp. 96–97

T. Igarashi, "On the Book of Journey through Architecture," *X–Knowledge Home*, vol. 20, p. 111

D. Nagasaka, "House in Sakai," *Shinkenchiku/Jutakutokushu*, 201, p. 151

S. Ohno, "Courtyard Designed by Waro Kishi," *Esquire*, vol. 17, 12, pp. 148–49

"10 Houses Designed by Architects," *Brutus*, vol. 24, 7, pp. 46–49

**2004**

K. Fridf, *Universalitet och Prototyp Japanska Rum*, Stockholm, pp. 198–218

S. Nakajima, "On Working Space," *Think*, 8, pp. 8–11

S. Ohno, "*Architect and his Car*," *Casa Brutus*, 52, p. 129

"Restaurant Wakuden," *Casa Brutus*, vol. 5, 6, p. 53

## Interviews

**1991**

Y. Takehara, O. Nakagawa, W. Kishi, "On Detail," *Shinjutaku*, vol. 46, 532, pp. 13–17

M. Ueda, "Conversation with Waro Kishi," *Kenchiku Bunka*, vol. 46, 535

**1992**

T. Narita, "On Recent Works," *Shitunai*, 453, pp. 60–63

**1993**

T. Hosono, "JIA (Japan Institute of Japan) Award for the Best Young Architect of the Year," *Nikkei Architecture*, 468, pp. 124–27

**1994**

S. Arakawa, N. Ueda, A. Kitagawara, K. Kitayama, T. Kimura, F. Tsukahara, H. Naito, N. Furuya, W. Kishi, "Body/Libido/Death," *Trance Chaos Tokyo*, Tokyo, pp. 128–55

T. Ashihara, H. Ohno, W. Kishi, "Architecture in the 21st Century," *Shinkenchiku*, vol. 69, 1, pp. 213–16

M. Ueda, M. Kawamukai, T. Watanabe, W. Kishi, "Renovation for the House of Modernism," *Kenchiku Magazine*, vol. 109, 1365, pp. 28–33

**1995**

M. Kawamukai, "Creation and Modernism," *Kensetsutsushin Shinbun*, November 13

O. Nakagawa, "Waro Kishi, Dream to technology exceeded the bounds," *P's circle*, 5, pp. 4–7

A. Roman, "Interview with Waro Kishi," *a+t*, 6, pp. 39–41

K. Tsuzuki, Waro Kishi, "On Tsuzuki Flat," *Shitunai*, 481, pp. 21–26, 47–49

R. Yamamoto, K. Sejima, Y. Futagawa, W. Kishi, "Architecture as a Dream," *GA Houses*, 47, pp. 74–87

**1996**

T. Endo, M. Motokura, H. Kimura, S. Takeyama, W. Kishi, "Houses and Landscape," *Shinkenchiku/Jutakutokushu*, 128, pp. 30–43

M. Kurokawa, W. Kishi, "Product Design and Architecture Design," *Tokyo Gas*, 53, pp. 6–11

Y. Nakamura, W. Kishi, "Contemporary Japanese Architecture," *Shinkenchiku*, vol. 71, 1, pp. 184–87

K. Nanba, W. Kishi, "On Modernism," *Jutaku-Kenchiku*, 259, pp. 158–63

Y. Nishizawa, W. Kishi, "Works of Kameki Tsuchiura," *Jutaku-Kenchiku*, 250, pp. 28–34

"The Prize of The Architectural Institute of Japan for Design," *Kensetsutsuchin Shinbun*, May 22

"The Prize of The Architectural Institute of Japan for Design," *Shinkenchiku/Jutakutokushu*, 122, p. 16

**1997**

F. Maki, S. Muramatsu, W. Kishi, "Towards New Vernacular," *Shinkenchiku/Jutakutokushu*, 129, pp. 24–37

H. Maruyama, "Interview with Waro Kishi," *SD*, vol. 390, pp. 39–40

J. Tanaka, W. Kishi, "Architecture as a Game," *Kenchiku Bunka*, vol. 52, 609, pp. 110–20

"Waro Kishi," *Arquine*, vol. 1, pp. 32–45

**1999**

Y. Futagawa, "Interview with Waro Kishi," *GA Japan*, 37, pp. 116–21

**2000**

H. Naito, W. Kishi, "On Architectural Design," *Shinkenchiku*, vol. 75, 5, pp. 60–67

"Architecture is architecture," *Space*, 21, pp. 96–101

**2001**

Y. Futagawa, "A Dialogue with Editor," *GA Houses*, 67, pp. 10–17

**2002**

"La Biennale di Venezia," *GA Japan*, 58, pp. 126–27

**2003**

M. Claesson, W. Kishi, "New Building," *Casa Brutus*, 39, p. 173

**2004**

K. Kojima, W. Kishi, "House as Architecture," *Shinkenchiku/Jutakutokushu*, 215, pp. 18–25

**Special thanks to**

**K. ASSOCIATES/Architects**
Miwa Tanabe
Yumiko Yamashita
Taku Araki
Asaco Takeuchi
Megumi Suzuki
Shingo Kitano
Kenichiro Yamase
Yushi Kojima
Naoko Miyamoto
Katsunobu Tasho
Takehiro Kitazawa
Kenichi Kishi
Masanaga Matsui
Miki Murakawa
Kozue Miyazaki
Ritsuko Toyama
Michiru Yoshida

**Kyoto Institute of Technology**
Kiyoshi Nakamura
Takuya Nakano
Ryu Mizumoto
Kenichi Hayama
Takayuki Ishitani
Takashi Hatano
Sachiyo Nakamura
Masashi Morimoto
Wakako Mori
Yasuko Tamai
Shingo Ozawa
Yusuke Sakai
Hidemitsu Takahashi
Yumiko Yonehara
Yousuke Inui
Tomoyuki Sakakida
Hideshi Abe
Kentaro Urai
Naonobu Wakisaka
Akihiro Nishizawa
Masahiro Kinoshita
Yu Sakuma
Junichi Nakai
Akio Hosoda
Koji Aiba
Hiroshi Ooyabu
Kana Hashimoto
Kohei Torigoe
Toshinori Oka
Hiroshi Tamura
Koji Haruna
Takashi Miki
Maki Yamakawa
Risa Yasubuchi
Kyouhei Aizono
Suguru Watanabe
Masataka Nakamura
Yukiko Tomita
Shinya Sato
Yuko Nakamura

**Collaborators**
Kim young–Sub + KUNCOOK
MOONHWA ARCHITECT
ASSOCIATES (Paju SW Office)

**Structural Engineer**
Urban Design Institute/Sadatoshi
Onimaru
Kyoto Institute of Technology Morisako
laboratory/Kiyotaka Morisako

**Mechanical Engineer**
Umeda Mechanical Design
Office/Kiyoshi Umeda

**Translators**
Alfred Birnbaum
Hiroshi Watanabe

**Photograph Credits**
The material illustrating this volume
was provided by the
K. ASSOCIATES/Architects studio
who have kindly granted permission
to publish it.
All remaining images, if not otherwise
specified, are by Hiroyuki Hirai.
Additional photos have been taken by:

Tetsuya Miura: p. 232

Kishi Lab., Kyoto Institute of
Technology: pp. 159, 163, 173

Hiroshi Ueda: pp. 181, 183, 184, 185

K. ASSOCIATES/Architects: p. 193

Nácasa&Partners Inc.: p. 211

Hisao Suzuki: p. 205


Holders of rights to any unidentified
photograph sources should contact
the publisher.